GOOD HOUSEKEEPING

GOOD
FOOD
Fast

D1450748

GOOD HOUSEKEEPING

GOOD FOOD

Fast

S U S A N N A   T E E

EBURY PRESS
LONDON

ACKNOWLEDGEMENT

I would like to extend a special 'thank you' to GOOD HOUSEKEEPING magazine for their assistance in providing a number of the recipes for inclusion in this book.

Published by Ebury Press
Division of the National Magazine Company Ltd
Colquhoun House
27-37 Broadwick St
London W1V 1FR

First impression 1987

ISBN 085223 602 6

Edited by Veronica Sperling
Art Direction by Frank Phillips
Designed by Bridgewater Associates
Photography by Simon Butcher
Styling by Sara Wyley
Cookery by Hilary Foster
Jacket photography by Bryce Attwell shows a variation of
Stir-Fried Beef with Vegetables (page 61)

Computerset by Stratatype Ltd, London
Printed in Great Britain at the University Press,
Cambridge

Contents

INTRODUCTION

This book is dedicated to all busy people who enjoy eating – and even cooking! – but who simply don't have the time to spend hours shopping and preparing food. Whether because of family commitments or a full-time job, or both, the pace of life today simply doesn't allow for lengthy stints in the kitchen.

The fact that we're in a hurry is reflected in our shopping habits. You only have to look in the butcher's or your local supermarket to see the huge range of time-saving cuts of meat on offer. There you will find pieces of well-trimmed, ready-boned meat on which there is no waste and which you can use right away. For example, you can buy cubed meat for skewers, strips cut thinly for stir-frying, boneless pork chops and pork tenderloin. And don't forget lamb neck fillets, which are excellent sliced and sautéed. We are also buying more chicken pieces than ever before – not surprising when you consider the wide choice of fillets, quarters, breasts, escalopes, thighs and drumsticks.

The recipes in this book are aimed to help you make the best use of both fresh ingredients and store-cupboard standbys to produce delicious dishes simply and quickly. Whether you are looking for a meal for the family, an impromptu supper dish to share with friends, or just a lunch time snack, your choice of recipe will depend on the time you have to prepare it. Simply look in the appropriate chapter to select a recipe which fits in with the amount of time you have at your disposal.

The times given for each chapter relate to the time taken from start to finish in completing each recipe. I've also allowed enough time to prepare a quick accompaniment. Even in Chapter 6, on Cooking Ahead, preparation and serving times have been kept to a minimum. The time involved is either in the marinating, cooking, chilling or freezing, when you can be doing something completely different.

With an eye to making life easier still, I have suggested suitable accompaniments in many cases, and have included a number of tips on how to cut corners without losing out on taste or quality.

I hope you enjoy the recipes in this book and that your busy lifestyle becomes a little less hectic!

STORE-CUPBOARD STANDBYS

With a carefully stocked store cupboard (and freezer) there's no need to be caught out when called upon for an instant meal and you'll be able to cope with any surprise situation. Many of the recipes included here can be whipped up in no time from ingredients you already have in store, including basic standbys such as eggs, cheese, milk, rice and pasta. Most of the recipes can use alternative ingredients, too. No tuna fish? Try canned salmon. Run out of spaghetti? Use any shape or size of pasta. Other recipes use store-cupboard ingredients and standbys that complement the fresh foods in the refrigerator. Try to be organised. Keep a notebook and pencil close at hand in the kitchen. If you use something, immediately add it to your shopping list so that you can replace it on your next shopping trip. Try also to plan meals ahead so that shopping is neither a haphazard nor a time-wasting affair.

Here is a list of suggested store-cupboard standbys. Some you should never be without!

THE STORE CUPBOARD

SAVOURY CANS Tomatoes (the most useful!); tuna; salmon; sardines; mackerel; anchovies; soups; sweetcorn kernels; pimientoes; artichoke hearts; red kidney beans; chick peas; lentils; butter beans; chilli beans.

SWEET CANS Fruits in natural or fruit juices; apple purée; creamed rice pudding; evaporated and condensed milk; chestnut purée.

SAVOURY JARS AND BOTTLES Green and black olives; gherkins; capers; preserved green peppercorns; a selection of oils, including olive and sunflower; a selection of vinegars; pesto; tomato ketchup; creamed horseradish; Worcestershire sauce; soy sauce; Tabasco; peanut butter; chutney; mayonnaise; a selection of mustards, including English and French, smooth and wholegrain.

SWEET JARS AND BOTTLES Honey; marmalade; jam; jellies; mincemeat; golden syrup.

MISCELLANEOUS DRIED AND LONG-LIFE GOODS Flours, plain and self-raising, wholemeal and white; cornflour; dried yeast; baking powder; powdered gelatine; custard powder; cocoa powder; varieties of sugar; nuts, including mixed chopped nuts, hazelnuts, walnuts, pine nuts, flaked, blanched and ground almonds; cereals, including unsweetened muesli, oats and oatmeal; dried fruits, including sultanas and no-soak apricots and prunes; glacé cherries; rice and pasta varieties; stock cubes; beans and pulses; dried mushrooms; long-life fruit juices; long-life milk; bread mixes and vacuum-packed breads; sweet and savoury biscuits; packet croûtons; teas and coffee.

DRIED HERBS AND SPICES Dried thyme; oregano; chives; tarragon; marjoram; basil; bay leaves; mint; parsley; mixed spice; cloves; nutmeg; cinnamon; vanilla pods (and essence); salt; black pepper; paprika; chilli powder; cayenne; coriander; turmeric; mustard powder; curry powder; ground cumin; sesame seeds and juniper berries.

FRESH HERBS If you have a garden or a window box do grow a few fresh herbs, as they make all the difference in flavour to a dish of steaming, lightly cooked vegetables, savoury butter or a freshly made omelette.

COOKING TIPPLES White and red wine; sherry; brandy; and your favourite liqueurs.

DAIRY PRODUCTS Butter and polyunsaturated margarine; natural yogurt (Greek style, too); long-life cream (some don't need refrigerating); eggs; hard cheeses, including a good Cheddar, a blue cheese and a soft cheese.

MISCELLANEOUS PRODUCTS Packets of bacon; sliced ham; salami; tubes of tomato purée, mixed herb purée and garlic purée; bottled lemon juice; plain chocolate; bread.

THE VEGETABLE RACK AND THE FRUIT BOWL Keep a selection of onions, potatoes, carrots and garlic in the vegetable rack, and oranges, apples and lemons in the fruit bowl with other seasonal fruits.

THE REFRIGERATOR

Keep all ingredients covered or well wrapped to prevent the flavours crossing from one to another. Cheeses will keep for a week or two but it's best to give them a few moments at room temperature before serving. Milk, cream and yogurts will keep for several days – often longer, but check date stamps when buying them. The same applies to cartons of fresh fruit juice. It's always useful to have a selection of salad ingredients, loosely wrapped in polythene bags. Unwashed, most will keep for a week. Once washed, dry them well before returning to the refrigerator in a polythene bag.

THE FREEZER Convenience foods, such as frozen vegetables, fresh orange juice, fresh pasta, some chicken joints and lamb chops, ice creams and peeled prawns, are always good standbys but keep a few unusual ingredients, too. Vol-au-vent cases, baked or uncooked, take little time to thaw or cook.

Listed below are some time-saving items which you might find useful to have readily available in the freezer. Choose those that you are most likely to need.

BREAD AND BREAD ROLLS Always a good standby to store. Sliced bread can be toasted straight from the freezer. Pitta (Lebanese) bread too will thaw under the grill. Crusty bread should not be stored in the freezer for more than 1 week as it tends to flake.

BREADCRUMBS Can be added frozen to onion sauce, stuffings and puddings which are to be cooked.

CASSEROLES AND STEWS Double the recipe and freeze half for later. Most can be reheated from frozen. It is important, though, to omit vegetables (such as potatoes) pasta and rice, that go mushy during freezing. Add them when you reheat the dish. Be careful when seasoning casseroles and curries for the freezer, as freezing strengthens flavours. When a dish has been cooked and cooled, remove surplus fat before freezing to avoid rancidity. There must be enough liquid in the dish to cover the meat completely, otherwise the meat may dry out. Casseroles must be cooled thoroughly and quickly before freezing. When reheating, it is important to bring the casserole to the boil and then simmer it for 15 minutes.

CHEESE Grate and freeze hard cheese in usable quantities. It can be used from frozen.

CHOCOLATE CURLS Add a professional touch to both puddings and cakes.

COFFEE BEANS They can be used from frozen.

CREAM Whipped double cream, piped into rosettes and then frozen, can be used to decorate puddings and cakes while still frozen. They take 10 minutes to thaw at room temperature. Sticks of frozen cream can be stirred straight into soups and sauces.

CROUTONS Fried bread croûtons can be reheated from frozen for 5-10 minutes in a hot oven. Use to garnish soups, salads and snacks.

FRESH HERBS Wrap and freeze whole sprigs and use them as they are, or crumble while still frozen to save time chopping. Alternatively, chop and freeze in ice cubes to drop straight into a dish during cooking.

ORANGE AND LEMON JUICE Freeze in small containers and use for drinks, cakes, dressings and sauces.

ORANGE AND LEMON RIND Store small quantities of grated rind and use for flavouring.

ORANGE AND LEMON SLICES Open freeze, then pack. Useful for garnishing foods and serving with drinks.

PASTRY All types will freeze well either as an uncooked dough or rolled out and baked. You can also freeze pastry unbaked in pies, quiches, tarts and flans. Make in bulk but pack in usable quantities. It may be more convenient to roll out raw pastry into pie lids, pie and flan cases and vol-au-vents before freezing.

SANDWICHES Prepare in bulk for parties or packed lunches.

SAUCES Make large quantities of sweet or savoury sauces and freeze in usable amounts.

SAVOURY BUTTERS Add a luxury touch to grilled meat, fish or vegetables. Use straight from the freezer.

SEVILLE ORANGES Buy when cheap and plentiful and freeze whole until you are ready to make marmalade.

SOUPS Make in large quantities and pack in usable amounts. Most can be reheated from frozen.

STOCK Make a large quantity, boil briskly to reduce, then freeze concentrated in small quantities for convenience.

TIPS FOR FAST COOKING

The following ideas will help you save precious minutes in the kitchen:

- Read the recipe through before commencing.
- Preheat the oven before starting.

■ Collect all the ingredients that you will need before you start cooking.

■ Heat the grill until really hot before using it.

■ Keep a set of measuring spoons handy. Hang them above the work surface rather than keeping them in a drawer where they are easily lost.

■ For good results and quicker results, use the right tools for the job. A good sharp cook's knife and a large chopping board are essential. Store them in a convenient place, too. Wooden spoons, for example, are useful stored, handles down, in a jar near the cooker.

■ If space allows and you own one, keep the food processor on the work surface.

■ Buy rinded bacon.

■ Don't bother to skin garlic cloves, they will crush straight through a garlic press. Incidentally, crushing rather than chopping garlic is quicker so do invest in a garlic crusher if you don't already have one. A sturdy metal one is better than plastic.

■ Buy freshly grated Parmesan cheese from a delicatessen and store it in a covered container in the refrigerator. Cartons of grated Parmesan are a poor substitute as far as flavour is concerned.

■ Make up a larger quantity of French dressing than needed (see the recipe on page 125) so that you always have some to hand when needed. Store it in a bottle or screw-topped jar.

■ Keep seasonings near the cooker so that they are handy for use.

■ For instant basting, brush a cod or haddock steak generously with French dressing (already stored in a screw-topped jar) before grilling.

■ For an instant garnish and decoration, buy a zester, currently my favourite tool! This marvellously efficient gadget takes off the outer peel of oranges and lemons in seconds and the long fine shreds look attractive on many sweet and savoury dishes.

■ Another useful gadget is a potato peeler with a U-shaped handle and swivel blade rather than one with an upright handle and swivel or fixed blade. It peels vegetables in minutes and is easy and comfortable to use.

■ Scissors are often useful and quicker for chopping than even the sharpest of knives. Use them for snipping bacon straight into the pan, and for cutting parsley, chives, smoked salmon and glacé fruit.

■ Chilled items can often be sliced or chopped more quickly than unchilled. Meat placed in the freezer for half an hour can be cut into thin slices or strips much more easily. Cucumber, tomato, peppers all slice better chilled.

■ Forget the old laborious making of a roux for white sauce – simply whisk all the ingredients together in the saucepan over a medium heat until the sauce thickens and comes to the boil. Simmer to cook as usual.

■ Have seasoned flour in a screw-topped jar or labelled flour dredger ready for action. When tossing meat in seasoned flour, put everything in a polythene bag and shake together.

■ Quickly jazz up a lamb chop by smearing redcurrant or mint jelly over the meat halfway through grilling.

■ Keep a bottle of ready squeezed lemon juice in the refrigerator. A handy measure to remember is that a juicy lemon gives about 3 tablespoons juice.

■ Small packs of savoury butters make wonderful instant garnishes, either during cooking or after.

QUICK VEGETABLES

These quick vegetable ideas will complement a main course yet take only minutes to prepare:

■ For courgette, carrot or celeriac shreds; using the coarse grater of a food processor, grate your favourite vegetable or a combination of vegetables into the bowl, then stir-fry them briskly in a large knob of butter and some oil until hot and barely cooked. Serve hot.

■ For speedily prepared mashed potatoes, the secret is to cut the peeled potatoes very small so they cook in half the time.

■ Jazz up plain boiled potatoes by cooking, draining and then tossing in a few tablespoons double cream, Greek strained yogurt or butter until lightly coated. Then sprinkle them with grated nutmeg, ground cinnamon, mace or chopped fresh herbs.

■ Stir-fry methods are both quick and delicious. Try shredded Chinese leaves, stir-fried in oil and then tossed in black bean and chilli sauce.

■ Save on washing up: parcel new potatoes, simply scrubbed, in foil with a garlic clove, knob of butter, salt and pepper. Oven cook for about 1 hour at 230°C (450°F) mark 8.

■ For instant Italian style courgettes, fry sliced courgettes in oil with a crushed garlic clove – it transforms them.

■ Make grilled tomatoes interesting by slicing them, then arranging the slices in a flame-proof dish and sprinkling with lemon rind and crushed garlic. Grill until hot. Alternatively, spread with some pesto sauce from a jar and grill. Another instant Italian treatment!

QUICK PUDDINGS

Here are some ideas for the sweet-toothed who get bored with just fruit:

■ Use a juicy pineapple (the aroma heightens when the fruit is ripe), cut into thick slices and decorate with halved strawberries anointed with orange liqueur.

■ Crush and fold meringues through thick Greek strained yogurt, spoon over fruit canned in natural juices.

■ Buy real dairy ice cream. Alternatively, if you eat a lot of ice cream, invest in an ice cream maker. Making ice cream in the freezer is a lengthy process but an electrical machine does the job in no time at all.

■ Black Forest trifles are exceptionally quick to prepare. Break up some trifle sponges and put in a serving bowl. Sprinkle with some kirsch or orange-flavoured liqueur. Spoon over a can of stoned cherries and top with whisked cream. Chill until ready to serve then decorate with chocolate curls.

■ Baked apples are a good, quick standby if you have the oven on. Core the apples, stand in a dish and stuff with mincemeat. Bake at 200°C (400°F) mark 6 for 40–60 minutes.

■ Cans of stewed apples take all the hard work out of laboriously having to peel and core apples for cooking. Use as a base for Apple Crumble (see page 123 for the topping). Other varieties of fruit can also be used.

■ Add grated orange rind to a can of stewed apples and use as a pie filling. It transforms it and is a quick alternative to preparing the fruit yourself.

■ The Danish dessert 'Peasant Girl with a Veil' is quickly made using a can of apple purée. Layer the apple with 175 g (6 oz) fresh breadcrumbs fried in 50 g (2 oz) butter until golden. Top with whipped cream.

■ For melon with port, cut a small Charentaise, Cantaloupe or Ogen melon (rock melon) in half. Scoop out the seeds, trim the bases so that they stand firmly and pour port into the centre. Serve!

EQUIPMENT TO MAKE LIFE EASIER

There are several electrical machines which are designed to make life easier and faster in the kitchen:

FOOD PROCESSORS A food processor is one of the most time-saving of all electrical appliances. Chopping onions and herbs, making breadcrumbs, grating cheese, puréeing soups and slicing vegetables can take up a lot of time when you are preparing food. Obviously all of these tasks can be done with manual tools but while these are fine for small quantities, a food processor does make life easier when more than the odd carrot or lump of sugar is involved. Some food processors have special attachments for whipping cream or egg whites. If you use your food processor a great deal, it is a good idea to buy an extra bowl to save having to keep washing up. When using a food processor, the secret is to leave the machine on the work surface. You're less likely to use it if it's stored away in a cupboard and you have to get it out and put it away every time.

In most of the recipes in Chapter 7 (Basic Recipes), and elsewhere where using a food processor will save time, I have given instructions for its use. Most of the dishes can be prepared without a food processor but in these cases you should obviously allow extra preparation time.

BLENDERS Blenders are marvellous for making batter, mayonnaise, pâtés, purées and soups. Some models can cope with dry ingredients, others require liquid before they can operate.

MIXERS Free-standing mixers take the toil out of mixing, blending, whisking, beating and creaming and they can take family-sized quantities of things like cake mixture which standard-sized food processors can't manage. Some mixers come with a liquidizer attachment which performs the same functions as a blender but does not have its own motor and is therefore not so powerful.

Hand-held mixers are compact and their great advantage is that they can be used with any size bowl – you can move the beaters around to ensure that all the ingredients are combined – and you can even use them over a pan on the hob, when making sauces for example.

ICE CREAM MAKER These are excellent for making delicious home-made ice creams and sorbets quickly and easily. They are ideal if you eat a lot of ice cream or would like to!

MICROWAVE COOKERS

A microwave is today's great saver of time and, if used to its best advantage, it can be a very useful appliance to have in conjunction with a conventional cooker. Quality ingredients are cooked speedily in a microwave and their flavour and texture are perfectly conserved. It is extremely useful for thawing those standbys you have in the freezer and reheats ready-made meals beautifully. A microwave gets on with one job while you're working on another, it axes the time spent doing jobs like softening butter and melting chocolate and above all it ensures good food gets from cooker to table quickly.

One of the great joys of a microwave is the way it cooks fish fast. Vegetables are also fabulous microwaved. With everything else ready, you don't have to think about them until minutes before eating. The beauty of microwaved vegetables is that they can be cooked in the dish they're to be served in. While cooking pasta by microwave is no time-saver, this is not the case where sauces are concerned and they have the advantage of coming to the table smooth and free of lumps.

Many of the recipes in this book can be prepared and/or cooked in a microwave and I've given instructions where appropriate. When cooking in a microwave, the times given for a recipe may well be even quicker than when using a conventional cooker.

30 TIPS TO MAXIMISE YOUR MICROWAVE

■ For a quick hot breakfast, serve porridge. Put the oats and milk in a bowl and cook on HIGH for 3–4 minutes, stirring occasionally.

■ Scrambled eggs are not only quick to prepare, but there's no messy saucepan to clean afterwards. Whisk the eggs, milk and butter together in a bowl and cook on HIGH for 3–5 minutes, whisking frequently.

■ Thaw frozen fish cutlets and fillets in their original wrappings, which should first be slashed.

■ Cook-in-the-bag fish such as kippers and smoked haddock can be cooked in their bags. Pierce the bag before cooking.

■ Small frozen vegetables such as peas and sweetcorn kernels can also be cooked in their plastic packets. Slit the top of the packet and shake it about halfway through the cooking to distribute the heat evenly.

■ Butter for spreading can be softened in the microwave on LOW for 30 seconds–1 minute.

■ Remember that bread can be warmed in the microwave. Place 4 rolls in a wicker serving basket and cook on HIGH for 20–30 seconds.

■ Melt butter or margarine in a ramekin dish to brush over foods.

■ Soften sugar that has become hard in the original wrapping on HIGH for 30–40 seconds.

■ Restore the texture to syrup or honey that has crystallised by cooking on HIGH for 1–2 minutes in its glass jar without the lid.

■ Plump up dried fruits by covering with water and cooking on HIGH for 5 minutes. Stir, leave to stand for 5 minutes, then drain well and dry on absorbent kitchen paper.

■ To toast flaked almonds, place them on a large plate and cook on HIGH for 8–10 minutes, stirring frequently.

■ Brown desiccated coconut in a roasting bag on HIGH for 5 minutes.

■ To remove the skins of hazelnuts and brown them, place in a single layer on absorbent kitchen paper and cook on HIGH for 30 seconds. Rub off the skins and microwave until just golden.

■ To roast chestnuts, slit the skins with a sharp knife and cook on HIGH for 3 minutes per 225 g (8 oz).

■ For quick roast potatoes, joints or whole poultry, start the cooking in a microwave oven, then brown and crisp them in hot fat or oil in a conventional oven or under a grill.

■ Use a microwave cooker for speedily cooking the basic ingredients for gratin and cheese-topped savoury dishes, then brown and crisp the surface under a conventional grill.

■ Prepare the fillings for pastry cases in a microwave cooker whilst the pastry is baking in a conventional one.

■ Tip baked beans on to buttered toast, flash in the cooker.

■ Release the maximum of squeezed juice from citrus fruits. Cook on HIGH for 1–2 minutes.

■ Take meat in portion sizes straight from the freezer and thaw for grilling while the vegetables are being microwaved.

■ For instant cooked aubergine (egg plant), prick all over and cook on HIGH for 12–15 minutes for one large aubergine.

■ Cut vegetables into a uniform size so that they cook evenly.

■ For magic trouble-free gelatine, leave the measured gelatine and liquid to swell for a few minutes. Put bowl in microwave and cook on HIGH for 30–50 seconds until dissolved, stirring frequently. Do not boil.

■ Steamed suet and sponge puddings cook in a fraction of the time needed for conventional steaming and the results are excellent. Follow your favourite recipe in a microwave cookery book.

■ Cook sauces in their serving jugs to cut down on washing up.

■ Reheat soups in individual bowls to save on washing up.

■ Frozen sauces and soups can be reheated straight from the freezer. Transfer to a bowl, then reheat, stirring to break up any frozen lumps.

■ Melt chocolate for puddings and cakes by breaking it into a bowl and cooking on LOW until it looks glossy and is soft on top. Then remove from the oven and stir gently until it is melted.

■ Sauces are excellent cooked in a microwave and there is little risk of lumps forming or burning occurring. Simply put the milk, butter, flour, salt and pepper in a bowl and cook on HIGH for 3–5 minutes, whisking frequently.

RECIPE NOTES

■ Follow either metric or imperial measures for the recipes.

■ All spoon measures are level.

■ Sets of measuring spoons are available in both metric and imperial sizes to give accurate measurement of small quantities.

■ Use size 4 (medium) eggs except when otherwise stated.

■ Use plain or self-raising flour unless otherwise stated.

■ Use brown or white breadcrumbs unless otherwise stated.

MICROWAVE COOKERY NOTES

IN THIS BOOK

■ HIGH refers to 100% full power output of 600–700 watts.

■ MEDIUM refers to 60% of full power.

■ LOW is 35% of full power.

■ If your cookery power output is lower than 600 watts, then you must allow a longer cooking time for all recipes in this book.

■ Add approximately 10–15 seconds per minute for a 500 watt cooker and 15–20 seconds per minute for a 400 watt cooker. No matter what the wattage of your cooker, always check food before the end of cooking time to ensure that it does not overcook.

■ Don't forget to allow for standing time.

BOWL SIZES

■ Small bowl = 900 ml (1½ pints)

■ Medium bowl = about 2.3 litres (4 pints)

■ Large bowl = about 3.4 litres (6 pints)

COVERING

■ Cook, uncovered, unless otherwise stated.

■ At the time of going to press, it has been recommended by the Ministry of Agriculture, Fisheries and Food that the use of cling film should be avoided in microwave cooking. When required to cover a dish, use a lid or plate, with a gap to let steam escape.

CHAPTER 1

5 – 10 MINUTES

WALNUT SOUP

Although this soup may sound unusual, it is quite delicious!
It also takes no more time than it would to open and heat
a can.

■

SERVES 4–6

1 garlic clove

175 g (6 oz) walnuts

600 ml (1 pint) chicken stock

150 ml (¼ pint) single cream

salt and pepper

■

1 Skin the garlic and put into a food processor or blender with the walnuts. Work until finely crushed. If using a blender you may need to add a little stock to blend the walnuts. Very gradually pour in the stock and blend until smooth.
2 Pour the soup into a saucepan and bring to the boil, stirring all the time. Remove from the heat.
3 Stir in the cream, reserving about 4 tablespoonfuls, salt and pepper. Serve hot, garnished with a swirl of the remaining cream on top.
■ TO COOK IN A MICROWAVE: Complete step 1. Pour the soup into a large bowl and cook on HIGH for 8–10 minutes until boiling, stirring occasionally. Complete the recipe.

TAPENADE

This is a delicious, pungent salty starter from Provence. In France it is served like a pâté, spread on slices of toasted French bread. It can also be served as a snack – simply accompany with halved, hard-boiled eggs. Cook the eggs while you are preparing the Tapenade.

■

SERVES 6–8
175 g (6 oz) stoned black olives
50 g (1¾ oz) can anchovy fillets, drained
1 small garlic clove
99 g (3½ oz) can tuna in oil
1 tablespoon lemon juice
1 tablespoon drained capers
1 teaspoon mustard powder
pepper

■

1 Put all the ingredients, including the tuna oil, in a blender or food processor and work until smooth. Transfer to a small bowl. Tapenade will keep in the refrigerator, covered, for up to 1 week.

THREE QUICK PATES

■

TUNA PATE

200 g (7 oz) can tuna fish, drained

100 g (4 oz) butter or margarine

1 teaspoon anchovy essence

squeeze of lemon juice

salt and pepper

■

POTTED CHICKEN

100 g (4 oz) cooked chicken

1 tablespoon lemon juice

pinch of dried tarragon

50 g (2 oz) butter or margarine

salt and pepper

■

SMOKED MACKEREL PATE

350 g (12 oz) smoked mackerel fillets

50 g (2 oz) butter or margarine

4 tablespoons mayonnaise

1 tablespoon lemon juice

pepper

■

1 Simply put all the ingredients in a food processor or blender and work until smooth. Turn into individual bowls or one large serving bowl and accompany with fingers of toast or French bread. They can all be served as a starter or snack.

HUMMUS

A food processor or blender is essential to make this traditional Middle Eastern dish. It is made with chickpeas and tahini which is a paste of sesame seeds sold in jars from health food shops and some supermarkets. Serve as a starter or snack, accompanied by warm pitta (Lebanese) bread.

■

SERVES 8
two 400 oz (14 oz) cans chickpeas
6 tablespoons lemon juice
150 ml (¼ pint) tahini
4 tablespoons olive oil
1 garlic clove
salt and pepper
lemon wedges, to garnish

■

1 Drain the chickpeas and put in a food processor or blender, reserving a few to garnish. Add the lemon juice and work to form a smooth purée.
2 Add the tahini paste, 2 tablespoons of the oil, crush in the garlic clove and season with salt and pepper. Work until smooth.
3 Spoon into a serving dish, sprinkle with the reserved chickpeas and oil and garnish with the lemon wedges. Serve with warm pitta (Lebanese bread).

POTTED SMOKED TROUT

WITH HORSERADISH

The two main ingredients of this dish have very individual flavours, but they complement one another beautifully. If using freshly grated horseradish – also available in jars – use only half the quantities given for the creamed variety.

■

SERVES 6
2 medium smoked trout
2 teaspoons creamed horseradish
100 g (4 oz) cream cheese
6 tablespoons soured cream or natural yogurt
1 tablespoon lemon juice
salt and pepper

■

1 Skin and bone the trout. Put the trout and all the remaining ingredients in a food processor or blender and work until smooth.
2 Spoon into individual dishes and serve either with toast or with French bread.

PITTA (LEBANESE BREAD) POCKETS

Toasted white or wholemeal pitta (Lebanese) bread is the perfect wrap-around for a hearty snack because you can so easily make it into a pouch. Grill the flatter side first and the bread will puff up well. Pitta keeps well in the freezer and is easy to toast from frozen. Once toasted, slice the pitta bread across the middle and stuff with one of the following fillings:

■

CHICKEN SALAD Combine cooked diced chicken, chopped celery, a few seedless green grapes cut in half and some pine nuts or chopped almonds with enough mayonnaise to bind the mixture together. Line the pitta with shredded lettuce and fill with the chicken salad.

EGG MAYONNAISE Combine chopped hard-boiled eggs with a little mayonnaise and add lots of snipped fresh chives and salt and pepper to taste. Line the pitta with shredded lettuce and fill with the egg mixture.

CHEESE, AVOCADO AND ALFALFA Spread the insides of the pitta with mayonnaise, then fill with grated cheese, alfalfa sprouts and avocado slices. Add a dollop of mayonnaise.

BACON AND TOMATO Spread the insides of the pitta with mayonnaise and fill with shredded lettuce, fried bacon slices and sliced tomatoes.

ROAST BEEF AND HORSERADISH Spread a thin coating of horseradish sauce on the insides of the pitta then fill with slices of roast beef and sliced tomatoes.

CHEESE AND HAM Spread a thin coating of pickle on the insides of the pitta then fill with sliced cheese, sliced ham and some crisp lettuce leaves.

HOT TOAST SNACKS

Almost anything can go on toast from simple poached eggs to luxury smoked salmon and scrambled egg. With today's array of different breads – crusty whites, nutty browns, soft baps (rolls), poppy-seeded rolls, sesame buns, pitta (Lebanese bread), muffins, crumpets – you can also ring the changes with the toasted base.
Invest in a sandwich toaster and you open up masses more possibilities. Go for fillings that stay moist, such as diced Mozzarella, tomato and green olives or crumbled Wensleydale and gherkin.

■

ONION RAREBIT Grate Cheddar or crumble Lancashire cheese, bind to a paste with milk and stir in snipped spring onion tops. Spread on to hot toast and grill until golden.

CELERY EGGS In a small pan, fry 1 small finely sliced celery stick in a little butter until soft but not browned. Crumble in 25 g (1 oz) Stilton or other hard blue cheese. Pile the cheese and celery mixture on one half of a toasted muffin. Grill until the cheese melts. Top with a poached egg and serve with the other muffin half, buttered.

CREAMED CHICKEN LIVERS Heat a large knob of butter in a pan, add chicken livers and seal quickly, shaking the pan occasionally. Cook until brown but still soft, then scatter a little flour over them. Cook for a further minute, then add a teaspoon of prepared mustard, a few tablespoons of single cream, salt and pepper. Heat gently, stirring, then pile on to hot toast.

CUCUMBER AND BLUE CHEESE TOASTIES Slice enough cucumber to give a good covering for each slice of bread. Toast bread – one side regular brown, second side pale. Overlap cucumber on the pale side of the toast, cover with slices of soft blue cheese and season. Grill until cheese begins to melt.

OMELETTE IN A ROLL Take a crisp finger roll, toast it inside, spread with cream cheese and slip in a one-egg herb omelette made with parsley, chives and tarragon.

FRIED HERRING ROES Dust soft herring roes in a little flour. Heat a large knob of butter in a pan and fry the roes until crisp and golden. Season and pile on to hot toast. Serve with lemon.

AVOCADO AND BACON Snip rashers of bacon into small pieces and fry until crisp. Meanwhile, mash half a small avocado and slice the remainder. Toast a slice of bread on both sides, then spread at once with the mashed avocado and top with the avocado slices. Season with salt and pepper. Add a dash of wine vinegar to the hot bacon fat, then spoon over the avocado and eat straight away. COX'S CHEESE AND NUT TOASTIES For each toastie, mix together 50 g (2 oz) grated Cheddar cheese, 1 grated small Cox's apple, a squeeze of lemon juice and a drop or two of Worcestershire sauce. Toast a slice of bread on both sides, then spread with the cheese mixture. Sprinkle a few chopped walnuts on top and grill for 3–4 minutes until golden brown.

FRENCH BREAD PIZZA

Cheese on toast is probably most people's favourite instant snack. This version makes a pleasant change. Vary the topping depending on the ingredients you have.

■

SERVES 2
100 g (4 oz) sliced salami
100 g (4 oz) Mozzarella, Bel Paese or Cheddar cheese
2 large tomatoes
1 small French loaf
butter or margarine, for spreading
a few black olives and anchovy fillets (optional)
pepper

■

1 Remove the rind and roughly chop the salami. Slice the cheese and chop the tomatoes.
2 Split the French bread in half lengthways. Lightly toast the crusty side.
3 Spread the untoasted side with butter. Top with the salami, tomatoes, cheese, olives and anchovies, if using. Cook under the grill until the cheese melts. Season and serve immediately.

GRILLED GOAT'S CHEESE
AND WALNUT SALAD

Packets of mixed lettuce leaves can be bought in many large supermarkets now. Those with a large cheese counter should sell goat's cheese, too. Serve as a starter or snack. It needs no accompaniment, except perhaps a glass of chilled white wine!

■

SERVES 4

50 g (2 oz) walnuts, roughly chopped

a selection of lettuce leaves such as radicchio, oak leaf, batavia, curly endive

4 tablespoons French dressing

two 100 g (4 oz) firm goat's cheeses, such as Chavignol

4 small slices of wholemeal bread

butter, for spreading

■

1 Preheat a grill. Spread the walnuts on a piece of foil. Wash and prepare the lettuce leaves and arrange on individual plates. Sprinkle over the French dressing.
2 Halve the goat's cheeses into 2 discs. Cut the crusts off the bread slices and toast one side until golden. Spread the untoasted side of the bread with butter, then place the cheese, cut side upwards, on the bread.
3 Grill for about 1 minute until the cheese just begins to bubble. Place on top of the lettuce.
4 Place the walnuts on their foil under the grill and cook for about 1 minute until heated through, stirring once or twice so that they do not burn. Sprinkle over the lettuce and serve at once.

WARM CHICKEN AND SPINACH SALAD

You can serve this warm salad as a light lunch or supper dish. As a variation to spinach, you may use shredded curly endive or fresh sorrel leaves if available. Accompany with warm French bread or bread rolls.

■

SERVES 2
2 chicken breast fillets, skinned
175 g (6 oz) young spinach leaves
3 tablespoons olive oil
small handful of pine nuts
small handful of sultanas
2 tablespoons white wine vinegar
salt and pepper

■

1 Cut the chicken into thin strips. Wash and dry the spinach, removing any coarse stalks.

2 Heat 2 tablespoons of the oil in a large frying pan and stir-fry the chicken for 2–3 minutes. Add the spinach and press down well. Cover and cook for about 1 minute until the leaves have just wilted.

3 Add the pine nuts and sultanas and toss together. Remove from the pan with a slotted spoon and transfer to 2 warmed serving plates.

4 Add the vinegar to the remaining oil in the pan, season with salt and pepper and stir well to combine. Pour the dressing over the salad and serve at once.

■ TO COOK IN A MICROWAVE: Complete step 1. Put the oil in a large bowl and cook on HIGH for 30 seconds. Add the chicken and cook on HIGH for 3–5 minutes, stirring occasionally. Add the spinach, cover and cook on HIGH for 30 seconds until wilted. Complete the recipe.

CHICKEN IN TUNA
FISH MAYONNAISE

This is a variation of the classic Italian dish, Vitello Tonnato, which is cold leg of veal coated in a tuna fish mayonnaise. Here cold cooked chicken is used in place of veal, or you can use turkey breasts. It is the perfect lunch dish for a hot summer's day. If time allows, prepare the dish the day before and chill in the refrigerator. This will allow the full flavour to develop.

■

SERVES 2–6
99 g (3½ oz) can tuna in oil
4 anchovy fillets
6 tablespoons mayonnaise
1 tablespoon lemon juice
1–2 tablespoons chicken stock, if necessary
pepper
2–6 cold cooked chicken breast fillets, skinned
capers, black olives, lemon wedges, to garnish

■

1 Put the contents of the can of tuna, anchovies, mayonnaise and lemon juice in a food processor or blender and work until evenly combined. If necessary, thin the mayonnaise mixture down to a coating consistency with a little chicken stock. Season with pepper. It is unlikely that you will need to add salt because of the saltiness of the anchovies.
2 Spoon over the chicken. Alongside, put a teaspoonful of capers, two or three olives and a lemon wedge to squeeze. Accompany with chunks of French bread.

FLAMBE BANANAS

Bananas are an instant packaged food! Adding the rum in the recipe makes it special but you can use lemon juice as an alternative. Serve with cream or vanilla ice cream.

■

SERVES 4
1 large orange
4 large bananas
knob of butter or margarine
½ teaspoon ground cinnamon
50 g (2 oz) demerara sugar (brown sugar)
4 tablespoons dark rum

■

1 Grate the orange and squeeze out the juice. Peel the bananas. Melt the butter in a frying pan and add the orange rind and juice. Stir in the cinnamon, then add the bananas and cook for a few minutes, until softened.
2 Add the sugar and stir until dissolved. Add the rum, set alight and stir gently to mix. Serve immediately.

THREE HOT SAUCES FOR ICE CREAM

■

CHOCOLATE SAUCE

MAKES about 300 ml (½ pint)

175 g (6 oz) plain chocolate, in pieces

large knob of butter

3 tablespoons milk

3 tablespoons golden syrup

■

1 Put all the ingredients in a small bowl, stand over a pan of warm water and heat gently, stirring, until the chocolate has melted and the sauce is warm.

■ TO COOK IN A MICROWAVE: In a medium bowl, cook the ingredients on HIGH for 3 minutes until melted, stir often.

■

WALNUT RUM SAUCE

MAKES about 450 ml (¾ pint)

175 g (6 oz) soft dark brown sugar

2 teaspoons instant coffee powder

6 tablespoons single cream or evaporated milk

knob of butter or margarine

1 tablespoon golden syrup

1 tablespoon rum

50 g (2 oz) walnuts, roughly chopped

■

1 Put all except the rum and walnuts in a saucepan and mix together. Cook over a low heat to dissolve the sugar, then simmer, stirring, for 2–3 minutes or until thickened slightly. Stir in the rum and the chopped walnuts. Serve warm.

■ TO COOK IN A MICROWAVE: Put all the ingredients except the rum in a medium bowl and cook on HIGH for 5 minutes, stirring occasionally until the sugar is dissolved and the sauce is slightly thickened. Add the rum.

OPPOSITE: PITTA (LEBANESE BREAD) POCKETS

page 25

■

TOFFEE SAUCE

MAKES about 300 ml (½ pint)
50 g (2 oz) caster sugar
125 g (4 oz) butter or margarine
150 ml (¼) pint double cream
50 g (2 oz) golden syrup
vanilla flavouring

■

1 Put the ingredients in a bowl over a pan of warm water and heat gently. Stir until melted and well mixed. Serve hot.
■ TO COOK IN A MICROWAVE: Put all the ingredients in a medium bowl and cook on HIGH for 2–4 minutes until hot and well mixed, stirring occasionaliy.

CINNAMON TOAST

This is for eating on a winter's afternoon when tea would be nice but you don't want to spend time in the kitchen.

■

SERVES 4
4 slices of bread
1 teaspoon ground cinnamon
2 tablespoons caster sugar
butter, for spreading

■

1 Toast the bread on one side only. Meanwhile mix the cinnamon and sugar together. Generously butter the untoasted side of the bread and sprinkle with the cinnamon sugar.
2 Grill until the mixture begins to melt. Cut into fingers and serve.

OPPOSITE: SKATE IN PEPPER BUTTER

page 50

TOASTED MUFFINS WITH
ROSE PETAL JAM

It is possible to make your own rose petal jam, but collecting enough rose petals is likely to be a lengthy business. Although the result is delicious, it does seem a shame to have to pick the roses when they are in full bloom and not put them in a vase. I've recently eaten tea at the Mandarin Hotel in Hong Kong (reputed to be the best hotel in the world!). They served toasted muffins with rose petal jam and I think this is how they make the jam. It was delicious, and made even more so by the atmosphere and service. What is more, this is certainly a quick version.

■

home-made or good quality strawberry jam

few drops of rosewater

muffins

butter, to serve

■

1 Spoon some strawberry jam into a china or glass jam pot, or small serving bowl. Stir in a few drops of rosewater to flavour.
2 Pull or cut the muffins open, then toast them with the two halves closed together again. This is the correct way to toast muffins rather than splitting them and toasting both halves which makes them tough. Toast them slowly so that the inside is warmed as well as the outside being toasted.
3 Serve the muffins split open, spread with butter, with the rose petal jam.

CHAPTER 2

10 – 15 MINUTES

GAZPACHO

Canned tomatoes, which have an excellent flavour, are used in this recipe to speed up preparation time. The secret is to season them well. Another short-cut is to use chilled tomato juice and ice cubes to save the usual chilling time.

■

SERVES 4
½ *small green pepper (capsicum)*
½ *small cucumber*
1 small onion
397 g (14 oz) can tomatoes
1 garlic clove
425 ml (15 fl oz) can tomato juice, chilled
2 tablespoons olive oil
2 tablespoons red wine vinegar
pinch of sugar
salt and pepper
ice cubes
1 packet of small croûtons

■

1 Remove the core and seeds from the green pepper (capsicum), then dice the flesh finely. Finely dice the cucumber, skin and finely dice the onion.
2 Reserve about 2 tablespoons of each of the chopped vegetables and put all the remaining vegetables in a food processor or blender. Add the tomatoes with their juice and crush in the garlic. Work to form a smooth purée.
3 Add the tomato juice, oil, vinegar, sugar, salt and pepper. Blend again until well mixed.
4 Pour the soup into a bowl and add the reserved chopped vegetables and a few ice cubes. Stir until the mixture is very cold. Serve, giving everyone an ice cube, and garnish with croûtons.

MOZZARELLA, TOMATO AND
AVOCADO SALAD

This is one of my favourite starters, as all my guests must now
know! It's also a delicious lunch-time snack served
with French bread.

■

SERVES 4
175 g (6 oz) Mozzarella cheese
4 medium tomatoes
2 ripe avocados
8 tablespoons French dressing
chopped fresh herbs, to garnish

■

1 Thinly slice the cheese and tomatoes and arrange at random on
four individual serving plates.
2 Halve the avocados lengthways, carefully remove the stones,
then peel and cut the avocados into slices. Arrange on the plates,
tucking the slices between the cheese and tomato slices.
3 Quickly spoon over the dressing to prevent the avocado from
discolouring. Garnish with chopped fresh herbs and serve with
warm French bread.

FLAGEOLET AND TUNA SALAD

There is such a wide variety of canned pulses available nowadays that it makes sense to keep a stock and vary their use. In this recipe, for example, you could also use red kidney beans or borlotti beans. Serve as a light meal.

■

SERVES 4

100 g (4 oz) shell pasta

salt and pepper

1 small onion

200 g (7 oz) can tuna in oil

260 g (9½ oz) can flageolet beans

6 tablespoons French dressing

black olives

chopped fresh herbs

■

1 Cook the pasta in plenty of boiling salted water for about 10 minutes until just tender.

2 Meanwhile, skin and very thinly slice the onion. Drain and flake the tuna. Drain the beans and rinse.

3 Drain the cooked pasta, rinse under cold water and drain well. In a salad bowl, toss the pasta with the onion, tuna, beans, French dressing, black olives, pepper and herbs.

■ TO COOK IN A MICROWAVE: Put the pasta and salt to taste in a large bowl. Pour over 600 ml (1 pint) boiling water. Stir, cover and cook on HIGH for 6–8 minutes until just tender, stirring occasionally. Leave to stand, covered, for 5 minutes. Meanwhile, complete the recipe.

Bulgur Salad

with Cheese and Herbs

Bulgur is whole wheat grain which has been boiled and baked and then cracked. It does not need cooking, simply soaking in water until the grains have swelled. For a cold salad, soak in cold water for 30 minutes. For a warm salad, soak in boiling water for 10–15 minutes. It is an ideal base for a salad, the most famous being the Lebanese Tabouleh which contains lots of parsley and mint. This recipe is a variation of that salad. With the addition of cheese it can be served as a light lunch or supper dish. If you have any over, it can be kept in the refrigerator and served cold.

∎

SERVES 4–6
175 g (6 oz) bulgur
100 g (4 oz) feta cheese
2 spring onions
4 tomatoes
3 tablespoons olive oil
salt and pepper
3 tablespoons lemon juice
2 tablespoons chopped fresh parsley

∎

1 Put the bulgur in a bowl and pour over 300 ml (½ pint) boiling water. Leave to soak for 10–15 minutes.
2 Meanwhile, cut the cheese into small cubes. Trim and finely chop the onions. Roughly chop the tomatoes.
3 Add the cheese, onions, tomatoes and remaining ingredients to the bulgur and toss well together. Serve warm.

BIG BARBECUE BURGERS

In supermarkets, you can now buy extra lean minced beef. It costs a little more than that containing more fat but it is well worth the extra expense. Flatten the burgers as you shape them – this way they will cook through more quickly.

■

SERVES 2
225 g (8 oz) lean minced beef
salt and pepper
2 tablespoons vegetable oil
2 tablespoons cider vinegar
1 tablespoon brown sugar
1 teaspoon prepared mustard
5 tablespoons tomato ketchup
hamburger rolls, salad ingredients and relish, to serve

■

1 Put the meat in a bowl and season with salt and pepper. Shape into 2 super-sized patties. Stir the rest of the ingredients together with 2 tablespoons water and spoon over the burgers.
2 Cook under the grill for 4–5 minutes on each side, brushing the burgers with the marinade during and after grilling.
3 Serve on lightly toasted hamburger rolls. Add lettuce, sliced tomatoes, sliced onion and relish.

SEVEN SAUCES FOR PASTA

Pasta is the perfect food for a quick meal and there is an increasingly wide choice of both fresh and dried varieties. Be adventurous and go for different flavours and colours and some of the more different shapes. Cook the pasta whilst preparing the sauce, or vice versa if cooking fresh pasta, and a meal can be on the table in no time at all.

For a main course, allow about 100 g (4 oz) dry or fresh pasta per person.

To cook pasta, always use plenty of boiling water with about 1 teaspoon salt to 1 litre (1¾ pints). Stir well, keep at a brisk bubble, uncovered, until al dente – firm, not soft. Dry pasta takes about 8–12 minutes after returning to the boil, fresh pasta only 2–3 minutes after returning to the boil. Drain well, then toss the hot pasta in a knob of butter or a little oil to prevent it sticking and then in your favourite sauce.

One of the best and fastest accompaniments for pasta is freshly grated Parmesan cheese, but with minimal effort you can easily ring the changes! Here are seven snappy sauces to try:

WALNUTS AND SAGE enough for 225 g (8 oz) pasta.

Heat 3 tablespoons oil in a saucepan, add 2 crushed garlic cloves and 4 rashers snipped streaky bacon. Fry for 5 minutes until softened. Stir in 50 g (2 oz) chopped walnuts, 1 tablespoon chopped fresh sage and 150 ml (¼ pint) soured cream and heat gently. Toss into hot pasta with grated Parmesan and freshly ground pepper.

SCALLOPS AND PINE KERNELS enough for 450 g (1 lb) pasta.

Heat 3 tablespoons oil and 2 whole skinned garlic cloves in a saucepan, but do not brown. Remove garlic, add 50 g (2 oz) pine kernels and cook until browned. Stir in 8 sliced scallops and cook until just opaque. Toss into hot pasta with about 25 g (1 oz) butter. Garnish the dish with a spoonful of chopped fresh basil.

CHEESE, GARLIC AND HERBS enough for 225 g (8 oz) pasta.

A short cut on sauces is to use a garlicky-herb soft cheese such as Boursin, Tartare or Roulé. Gently heat a 142 g (5 oz) packet or piece of cheese in a saucepan with a generous splash of double cream until the cheese has melted. Toss with hot pasta. Finish with a generous sprinkling of freshly grated Parmesan and freshly ground pepper.

COURGETTES WITH TOMATO OR PESTO SAUCE It is worth looking at the ready-made sauces in jars on grocers' shelves. There are several acceptable tomato sauces and pesto, the Italian sauce made from fresh basil, garlic, olive oil, Parmesan cheese and pine nuts, is always wonderful served over freshly cooked pasta. Cook pasta in boiling water and for the last minute add sliced courgettes, about 1 per person. Drain, then toss in tomato or pesto sauce. Finish with grated Parmesan cheese.

HAM AND MUSHROOM SAUCE enough for 225 g (8 oz) pasta.

Melt 50 g (2 oz) butter in a saucepan, add 100 g (4 oz) sliced mushrooms and fry for 2–3 minutes. Add 2–4 slices smoked ham, cut into fine strips, a little freshly grated nutmeg, salt and pepper. Stir in 150 ml (¼ pint) double cream and simmer for 2 minutes. Toss with hot pasta and finish with grated Parmesan cheese.

CLAM SAUCE enough for 225 g (8 oz) pasta.

In a saucepan, heat a 439 g (15 oz) can clams in brine with their juice with 1–2 crushed garlic cloves – clams toughen if heated too long. Swirl a little olive or sunflower oil through hot drained pasta until it glistens. Toss in the clams and their juices with lots of chopped fresh parsley and freshly ground black pepper. Serve with grated Parmesan cheese and lemon wedges.

HOME-MADE TOMATO SAUCE enough for 450 g (1 lb) pasta.

This is a quick recipe for tomato sauce as it uses a can instead of fresh tomatoes. Nevertheless, with plenty of seasonings, none of the flavour is sacrificed. All you lose are the time-consuming jobs of skinning the tomatoes and sieving the sauce. In the bowl of a food processor, fitted with a metal blade, put 1 small skinned onion and 1 whole skinned garlic clove and work until finely chopped. Add 1 teaspoon tomato purée, a pinch of dried basil, a pinch of sugar, 1 tablespoon olive oil, salt and pepper. Work until smooth. Heat in a saucepan for 10-15 minutes until slightly thickened. Toss with hot pasta and finish with freshly grated Parmesan cheese.

MEXICAN TACOS

Mexican taco shells can be bought in a packet. Warmed and then filled with a variety of fillings, spicy hot tacos are an ideal snack to be eaten with the fingers.

■

Mexican taco shells

shredded lettuce

Chicken, Guacamole or Mexican chilli beans and pork filling (see below)

■

1 Put the taco shells in the oven to warm according to the instructions on the packet, then add a little shredded lettuce and one of the following fillings:

CHICKEN Fry 1 chopped onion until soft, then add chopped tomatoes, shredded cooked chicken, salt and pepper and heat through. Add a little shredded lettuce to the taco shells, spoon in the chicken mixture, add a few drops of Tabasco, then serve.

GUACAMOLE Mash 2 small avocados with a squeeze of lemon juice then add 2 skinned and chopped tomatoes, 1 small finely chopped onion, 1 tablespoon chopped fresh coriander or parsley, 1 seeded and finely chopped green chilli, salt and pepper. Add a little shredded cooked chicken to the taco shells and top each with 1–2 tablespoons of the dip.

PORK WITH CHILLI BEANS See the recipe on page 104. Chop the pork rashers into small pieces and add 1–2 tablespoons of hot chilli beans and the pork to each taco shell and top with grated Cheddar cheese.

CROQUE MONSIEUR

This tasty fried cheese and ham sandwich is an ideal quick snack and is sold in cafés all over France. Croque Monsieur is the classic recipe but there is another version called Croque Madame which is similar except that it is served topped with a poached egg. Gruyère is the correct cheese to use but in France it is possible to buy packets of processed 'Croque Monsieur' cheese slices which come already cut to shape. Outside France, you can use any processed slices or even Cheddar cheese which is less expensive than Gruyère.

■

SERVES 1
2 slices of white bread
knob of butter
1 slice of cooked ham
40 g (1½ oz) Gruyère cheese
salt and pepper
1 tablespoon vegetable oil

■

1 Cut the crusts off the bread, then spread 1 side of each slice with some butter.
2 Place the ham on the buttered side of 1 slice of bread, cutting it to fit if necessary. Repeat with the Gruyère cheese. Sprinkle with salt and pepper, then top with the remaining slice of bread, buttered side down.
3 Press the sandwich together firmly, then cut into 4 triangles and press the edges together.
4 Melt the remaining butter with the oil in a frying pan, add the 4 triangles and fry over a medium heat until crisp and golden on both sides. Press with a fish slice to keep the sandwiches together and turn once during frying. Serve hot. Accompany with a green salad if liked.

EGGS IN SAUCE VERTE

Eggs are the original convenience food when it comes to quick, light, satisfying meals. Here they are made to look and taste particularly delicious by the addition of a glistening green sauce.

■

SERVES 2
1 medium leek
large handful watercress sprigs
pinch of ground coriander
knob of butter
salt and pepper
4 eggs
1 tablespoon Greek strained yogurt or fromage blanc
grated Parmesan cheese

■

1 Trim and slice the leek and wash well. Reserve a few watercress sprigs to garnish. Put the remaining watercress sprigs, without any coarse stems, in a saucepan with the leek, coriander, butter, salt, pepper and 4 tablespoons water. Cover and cook until the watercress has collapsed.

2 Meanwhile, soft-boil the eggs in boiling water for 6 minutes. Remove the shells under cold water.

3 Put the watercress in a food processor or blender and work until smooth. Stir in the yogurt.

4 Serve the eggs in warm dishes with the hot sauce, dusted with Parmesan and garnished with the reserved watercress sprigs. Accompany with crusty bread.

■ TO COOK IN A MICROWAVE: Put the watercress sprigs, leek, coriander, butter, salt, pepper and water in a large bowl. Cover and cook on HIGH for 5 minutes until the watercress has collapsed. Complete the recipe.

CHEESE FONDUE

Cheese fondue must be one of the quickest dishes to prepare because in fact it is traditionally cooked at the table, so all you have to do is collect the ingredients together, grate the cheese and cut the bread. You can even get someone else to do the stirring! It's nice for a family meal and fun to serve for an informal supper party. The traditional Swiss cheeses can be replaced with mature Cheddar cheese for a less expensive version. When entertaining, small glasses of kirsch can be served with the fondue – guests should dip the cubes of bread first in the kirsch, before dipping them in the fondue.

■

SERVES 4

225 g (8 oz) Gruyère cheese

225 g (8 oz) Emmenthal cheese

4 teaspoons cornflour

pepper

whole nutmeg

French bread, to serve

1 garlic clove

300 ml (½ pint) dry white wine

splash of kirsch (optional)

■

1 Coarsely grate the cheeses, then toss with the cornflour, pepper and a pinch of freshly grated nutmeg.
2 Cut the bread into cubes and pile into a basket.
3 Skin the garlic and use to rub the inside of a fondue pot or flameproof dish.
4 Place the fondue dish over a fondue burner on the table. Pour in the wine, add the cheese mixture and heat gently, stirring all the time, until the cheese has melted and the mixture is of a smooth, thick consistency. Add the kirsch, if using.
5 The fondue is now ready for serving. Accompany with the cubes of French bread and provide long forks on which to spear the bread to dip it in the fondue.

Raclette

This is another traditional Swiss dish which is as quick to make as cheese fondue. In Switzerland it is made by holding a large piece of Raclette cheese over an open fire and scraping off the melted cheese. It is served with hot, boiled new potatoes, pickled cucumbers and cocktail onions. Electric Raclette machines in which to melt the cheese can be bought in this country or you can improvise by melting the cheese in an oven. Ask for Raclette cheese in specialist food shops and cheese shops. Gruyère cheese can be use as an alternative.

■

SERVES 4

450 g (1 lb) Raclette cheese

pepper

boiled new potatoes, pickled cucumbers and cocktail onions, to serve

■

1 Cut the rind off the cheese and slice the cheese finely.
2 Put the slices, slightly overlapping, in a buttered shallow ovenproof dish and bake at 190°C (375°F) mark 5 for about 5 minutes until the cheese has melted and the surface is smooth.
3 Sprinkle with pepper and serve in the cooking dish to keep it hot. Accompany with boiled new potatoes, pickled cucumbers and cocktail onions.

PASTA SALAD WITH
AVOCADO DRESSING

Avocados are an ideal quick convenience food to serve as a starter or snack. Cut in half, remove the stone and serve simply filled with French dressing. Alternatively, they combine beautifully with fish. Bind some prawns or white crab meat with a little mayonnaise and pile into the centre. Crispy bacon is another good combination. Here avocados are used as a dressing for a pasta salad with bacon.

■

SERVES 4
225 g (8 oz) pasta shapes
salt and pepper
175 g (6 oz) mange-tout (snowpeas)
8 rashers rindless streaky bacon
1 tablespoon vegetable oil
2 ripe avocados
4 tablespoons natural yogurt
1 garlic clove
Tabasco

■

1 Cook the pasta in boiling salted water for about 10 minutes until tender. Meanwhile, top and tail the mange-tout (snowpeas) and add to the pan of cooking pasta.
2 Snip the bacon into pieces and fry in the oil for about 5 minutes until crisp and golden brown.
3 Halve one of the avocados, remove the stone, then scoop out and mash the flesh. Mix quickly with the yogurt, crushed garlic, a few drops of Tabasco, salt and pepper. Chop the remaining avocado into small pieces.
4 Drain the pasta and mange-tout well, rinse in cold running water and drain again. Stir the pasta into the sauce and toss in the bacon and chopped avocado. Serve at once or the avocado dressing may discolour.

OPPOSITE: PRAWNS AND ARTICHOKES WITH BUTTERED TAGLIATELLE

page 52

CALF'S LIVER IN CREAM SAUCE

This Swiss recipe should be made with calf's liver but you can use lamb's liver if you prefer.

■

SERVES 2
1 tablespoon flour
½ teaspoon paprika
4 slices of calf's liver, weighing about 225 g (8 oz)
knob of butter
2 tablespoons dry white wine
4 tablespoons single cream
1 tablespoon chopped fresh parsley
salt and pepper

■

1 Put the flour in a polythene bag and add paprika to season. (Do not add salt as this will toughen the liver.) Add the liver and shake well to coat each piece.

2 Heat the butter in a frying pan. Add the liver and fry over medium heat for 2–3 minutes on each side. Remove from the pan and place on warmed serving plates.

3 Add the wine to the pan and boil briskly for 1 minute, stirring in any sediment from the bottom of the pan. Lower the heat, stir in the cream and parsley and season with salt and pepper.

4 Heat gently without boiling, then spoon over the liver. Serve hot with buttered noodles and a green vegetable.

■ TO COOK IN A MICROWAVE: Complete step 1. Put the butter in a shallow dish and cook on HIGH for 45 seconds until melted. Add the liver and microwave on HIGH for about 5 minutes or until the liver changes colour. Remove from the dish and place on warmed serving plates. Add the wine to the dish and microwave on HIGH for 2 minutes, stirring occasionally. Stir in the cream, parsley, salt and pepper and microwave until hot but not boiling, then spoon over the liver.

OPPOSITE: WARM SCALLOP, BACON AND CROUTON SALAD

page 57

SKATE IN PEPPER BUTTER

Skate is so often overlooked, which is a pity because it's a delicious fish, is quick and simple to prepare and has no unwelcome fine bones.

∎

SERVES 4
2 skate wings
salt
2 tablespoons black peppercorns
75 g (3 oz) butter
1 garlic clove
1 teaspoon chopped fresh sage

∎

1 Cut each skate wing in half. Put the fish in a roasting tin and cover with salted water. Bring to the boil, then simmer for 10–15 minutes, until tender.
2 Meanwhile, crush the peppercorns. Melt the butter in a saucepan, add the peppercorns and crush in the garlic. Stir over a medium heat for about 1 minute until the butter is golden brown. Add the chopped sage.
3 Drain the cooked fish and serve at once with the pepper butter poured over. Accompany with mange-tout (snowpeas) and small boiled new potatoes.
∎ TO COOK IN A MICROWAVE: Weigh the fish. Cut each skate wing in half. Put 25 g (1 oz) of the butter in a large shallow dish and microwave on HIGH for 45 seconds until melted. Arrange the skate in the dish, cover, and cook on HIGH for 4 minutes per 450 g (1 lb). Turn the skate over and reposition the pieces halfway through the cooking. Meanwhile, crush the peppercorns. Remove the skate and place on warmed serving plates. Add the remaining butter to the dish and cook on HIGH, uncovered, for 1 minute until melted. Add the peppercorns, crush in the garlic and add the sage. Cook on HIGH for about 2 minutes, stirring once. Pour over the fish and serve.

Mussels in Cream and Garlic Sauce

Fresh mussels are time-consuming to prepare so this recipe uses frozen ones. You will hardly notice any loss in flavour – only the lack of shells! They should be thawed before cooking. Serve as a special main course.

■

SERVES 2
large knob of butter
1 garlic clove
generous splash of dry white wine
150 ml (¼ pint) double cream
pinch of saffron strands or ground turmeric
1 tablespoon lemon juice
salt and pepper
450 g (1 lb) frozen mussels, thawed
chopped fresh parsley, to garnish

■

1 Melt the butter in a saucepan, crush in the garlic and fry for 1 minute. Add the wine and boil rapidly for 2–3 minutes until reduced.

2 Add the cream, saffron or turmeric and boil rapidly again until reduced and thickened. Add the lemon juice, salt, pepper and mussels and cook for 2–3 minutes to heat through.

3 Serve at once, sprinkled with chopped fresh parsley. Accompany with chunks of French bread to mop up the garlic sauce.

■ TO COOK IN A MICROWAVE: Put the butter in a large bowl and cook on HIGH for 30 seconds or until melted. Crush in the garlic and cook on HIGH for 1 minute. Add the wine and cook on HIGH for 2 minutes until reduced. Add the cream, saffron or turmeric and cook for a further 2 minutes until reduced. Add the mussels and lemon juice and cook on HIGH for 2–3 minutes until just heated through. Season with salt and pepper, garnish with parsley and serve at once.

PRAWNS AND ARTICHOKES WITH
BUTTERED TAGLIATELLE

Prawns with artichokes make a superb dinner à deux at home.
The prawns can be cooked from frozen but make sure they
are thawed before adding the other ingredients.

■

SERVES 2
225 g (8 oz) dried tagliatelle
salt and pepper
1 medium onion, skinned and thinly sliced
225 g (8 oz) tomatoes
6 stuffed green olives
200 g (7 oz) can artichoke hearts, drained
1 tablespoon olive oil
250 g (8 oz) frozen cooked peeled prawns
1 teaspoon chopped fresh or *¼ teaspoon dried thyme*
1 lemon
large knob of butter

■

1 Cook the tagliatelle in a large saucepan of boiling salted water
for 8–12 minutes until al dente – firm, not soft. Meanwhile,
quarter the tomatoes. Halve the olives and the artichoke hearts.
2 Heat the oil in a frying pan. Add the prawns, onion and thyme
and grate in the rind from the lemon. Cook over medium heat,
stirring, for 3–4 minutes until the prawns have thawed.
3 Stir in the tomatoes, olives and artichoke hearts and cook for a
further 2–3 minutes or until hot. Season with salt and pepper.
4 Drain the tagliatelle well, return to the hot saucepan and toss
with the butter. Serve the prawns and artichokes on top.
■ TO COOK IN A MICROWAVE: Complete steps 1 and 2. Put the oil,
prawns, onion, thyme and grated lemon rind into a large bowl.
Cook on HIGH for 5 minutes until the prawns have thawed,
stirring frequently. Stir in the tomatoes, olives and artichoke
hearts and cook on HIGH for a further 2 minutes until hot.
Season with salt and pepper. Complete step 5.

ZABAGLIONE

Serve this rich classic Italian dessert when entertaining.

∎

SERVES 6
4 egg yolks
65 g (2½ oz) caster sugar
100 ml (4 fl oz) Marsala

∎

1 Put the egg yolks and sugar in a large heatproof bowl. Using an electric whisk, whisk together, then add the Marsala and whisk until mixed.
2 Place the bowl over a saucepan of simmering water and heat gently, whisking the mixture until it is very thick and creamy.
3 Pour the zabaglione into six glasses and serve immediately, with sponge fingers or paper-wrapped macaroon biscuits.

PEACH SOUFFLE OMELETTE

It's almost like magic that soufflé omelettes puff up and don't fall apart. To help fold this puffy omelette, first make a shallow cut across the centre.

■

SERVES 2

2 fresh ripe peaches

1 tablespoon Grand Marnier

4 eggs

2 teaspoons caster sugar

about 25 g (1 oz) butter

■

1 Halve and slice the peaches, put in a bowl and add the Grand Marnier.
2 Separate the eggs. Beat the egg yolks and sugar together with a wooden spoon until light in colour. Whisk the egg whites until stiff but not dry. Fold into the yolk mixture.
3 Heat the butter in a large frying pan. When foaming, pour in the egg mixture and cook over a medium heat until the underside is golden and set.
4 Flash under the grill until golden and set on top. Spoon the peaches and juices on to one half. Grill again to warm through.
5 Fold the omelette, cut in half and serve on warmed plates. Eat immediately.

CHAPTER 3

15 – 20 MINUTES

BAKED EGGS IN BUTTERCRISP CASES

These are lovely for breakfast or a light lunch or supper dish.
As a quick alternative to pastry, I've used slices of bread.
Baked with butter, they are beautifully crisp.

■

MAKES 2
2 large thin slices of white bread
butter, for spreading
2 eggs
freshly grated Parmesan cheese
salt and pepper

■

1 Using a pastry cutter, cut the bread into rounds large enough to
fit two individual Yorkshire pudding tins. With a rolling pin, roll
out more thinly and flatten.
2 Spread quite thickly with butter and press the slices, buttered
sides down, into the tins.
3 Break an egg into each. Sprinkle a little grated cheese on top
and season with salt and pepper.
4 Bake at 190°C (375°F) mark 5 for about 10 minutes until the eggs
have set. Serve hot.

WARM SCALLOP, BACON AND
CROUTON SALAD

Frozen scallops, sold out of the shell, are available from high-class fishmongers, but ask your fishmonger if you can have shells for serving. Scald them in boiling water and scrub them before use. Serve this salad as a starter or light main course.

■

SERVES 4–6
a selection of lettuce leaves such as radicchio, oak leaf, batavia, curly endive
4 tablespoons French dressing
12 large scallops
8 rashers streaky bacon
2 tablespoons vegetable oil
25 g (1 oz) butter
1 packet small croûtons

■

1 Wash and prepare the lettuce and arrange in scallop shells or on individual plates. Sprinkle over the French dressing.

2 If necessary, remove and discard the tough white 'muscle' from each scallop. Separate the corals from the scallops and set aside. Cut the white part into fairly thick slices. Cut the bacon into thin strips.

3 Heat the oil and butter in a frying pan and fry the bacon for 5 minutes until soft. Add the scallops and fry for a further 5 minutes until the bacon is crisp and the scallops tender. Do not overcook the scallops or they will become tough and rubbery. Stir the corals and croûtons into the pan during the final 2–3 minutes of the cooking time.

4 Turn on to the lettuce and serve at once.

■ TO COOK IN A MICROWAVE: Complete steps 1 and 2. Heat a large browning dish on HIGH for 5–8 minutes or according to manufacturer's instructions, adding the oil and butter for the last 15 seconds. Without removing the dish from the oven, add the bacon and cook for 2 minutes. Stir in the scallops and cook for 2–3 minutes until tender. Stir in the corals and croûtons and cook for a further 1 minute until hot, then turn on to the lettuce.

SPICY CHICKEN SALAD WITH

CASHEW NUTS

Most people are familiar with one or another version of the ubiquitous recipe for Coronation Chicken – diced cold chicken tossed in a curried apricot mayonnaise – created by the Cordon Bleu school in London in honour of the coronation of Queen Elizabeth II. This recipe is a variation of that dish. It is quick and simple to make and delicious for a summer lunch or supper. Simply accompany with a cucumber salad.

■

SERVES 4
150 ml (¼ pint) mayonnaise
2 teaspoons curry paste
1 teaspoon tomato purée
1 teaspoon lemon juice
pinch of chilli powder
salt and pepper
4 cold cooked chicken breast fillets
50 g (2 oz) cashew nuts

■

1 In a large bowl, stir together the mayonnaise, curry paste, tomato purée, lemon juice, chilli powder, salt and pepper.
2 Remove the skin from the chicken and cut the flesh into shreds. Add to the sauce and toss together. Turn on to a serving dish.
3 Spread the cashew nuts on a piece of foil and place under the grill. Cook for 1–2 minutes until toasted, stirring once or twice so that they do not burn. Sprinkle over the chicken and serve.

SHREDDED SESAME CHICKEN
WITH PEPPERS (CAPSICUMS)

Serve this Chinese stir-fry for a quick evening meal. Once the ingredients are prepared, it only takes a few minutes to cook. Chinese egg noodles or rice are the most suitable accompaniment.

■

SERVES 4
4 chicken breast fillets, skinned
1 large red pepper (capsicum)
1 large yellow pepper (capsicum)
6 spring onions
2.5 cm (1 inch) piece of fresh root ginger
225 g (8 oz) can sliced bamboo shoots
2 tablespoons vegetable oil
2 tablespoons sesame seeds
2 tablespoons soy sauce
2 tablespoons dry sherry

■

1 Cut the chicken into thin strips. Cut the peppers (capsicums) into thin strips, discarding the core and seeds. Trim and slice the spring onions. Peel and coarsely grate the ginger. Drain the bamboo shoots.

2 Heat the oil in a wok or large frying pan. Add the chicken and stir-fry for 3 minutes.

3 Add the prepared vegetables and ginger and stir-fry for 2 minutes. Add the sesame seeds and stir-fry for a further minute.

4 Add the soy sauce and sherry. Bring to the boil and boil for 1 minute, stirring all the time. Serve at once.

■ TO COOK IN A MICROWAVE: Complete step 1. Put all the ingredients in a large bowl and stir well to mix. Cook, uncovered, on HIGH for 5–6 minutes until the chicken is tender and the vegetables are tender but firm, stirring occasionally. Serve hot.

DUCK BREASTS

WITH BLACKCURRANT SAUCE

Individual portions of duck are ideal for frying. Duck combines beautifully with fruit, as devotees of the classic Duck with Orange already know. Here I have used blackcurrants but you can use raspberries as an alternative.

■

SERVES 2
large knob of butter
2 tablespoons vegetable oil
2 duck breasts, with skins on
1 tablespoon wine vinegar
2 tablespoons dry white wine
213 g (7½ oz) can blackcurrants in unsweetened fruit juice
salt and pepper

■

1 Heat the butter and oil in a frying pan. Add the duck breasts, skin side down, and fry over high heat for 2–3 minutes. Turn the breasts over and cook for a further 5 minutes until tender.
2 Slice the duck breasts neatly, then arrange on warmed plates.
3 Add the vinegar to the pan and boil rapidly for 1 minute, stirring in any sediment from the bottom of the pan. Stir in the wine. Lower the heat and stir in the blackcurrants with their juice. Season with salt and pepper.
4 Heat gently, then pour the sauce over the duck. Serve hot with boiled new potatoes and a salad or a green vegetable.
■ TO COOK IN A MICROWAVE: Heat a large browning dish on HIGH for 5–8 minutes or according to manufacturer's instructions, adding the oil for the last 15 seconds. Without removing the dish from the oven, add the duck breasts, skin side down, and cook on HIGH for 6–7 minutes or until tender, turning the duck once. Complete step 2. Add the vinegar to the dish, stirring in any sediment from the bottom of the dish. Cook on HIGH for 2 minutes until boiling. Stir in the wine, blackcurrants with their juice, salt and pepper. Cook on HIGH for 2–3 minutes until hot. Spoon the blackcurrant sauce over the duck and serve hot.

STIR-FRIED BEEF WITH VEGETABLES

Stir-fry dishes are quick to make. This recipe uses fresh vegetables but for an even speedier dish you can use a packet of ready-prepared stir-fry vegetables which are now sold in most large supermarkets. You can also vary the vegetables and use, for example, chopped celery or baby sweetcorn and substitute almonds for the walnuts. I've also used quick-fry steak for this recipe. These are slices of lean cuts of beef which have been passed between knife-covered rollers to tenderise them for easy frying.

■

SERVES 2
225 g (8 oz) quick-fry steak
100 g (4 oz) mange-tout (snowpeas)
100 g (4 oz) mushrooms
4 spring onions
2 medium carrots
3 tablespoons vegetable oil
1 tablespoon soy sauce
2 tablespoons hoisin sauce
2 tablespoons dry sherry
small handful of broken walnuts

■

1 Thinly slice the steak. Top and tail the mange-tout (snowpeas). Slice the mushrooms. Trim and slice the spring onions. Scrub and slice the carrots into matchstick strips.
2 Heat the oil in a wok or large frying pan. Add the steak and carrots and stir-fry for 2–3 minutes, tossing them all the time. Add the mange-tout, spring onions and mushrooms and stir-fry for a further 1–2 minutes until lightly browned.
3 Stir in the soy sauce, hoisin sauce and sherry. Bring to the boil and boil for 1 minute. Sprinkle over the walnuts and serve hot with egg noodles, boiled rice or pasta.

SAUTEED VEAL WITH
MUSTARD AND CREAM

These strips of veal escalope with a creamy sauce make a good main course for a midweek supper party when you are short of time. Use wholegrain mustard as specified in the recipe as this is less strong than some of the smooth English and Dijon mustards which would completely overpower the delicate flavour of the dish.

■

SERVES 4
4 veal escalopes, about 100–175 g (4–6 oz) each
40 g (1½ oz) butter
150 ml (¼ pint) chicken stock
150 ml (¼ pint) single cream
1 tablespoon wholegrain mustard
2 tablespoons lemon juice
salt and pepper
chopped fresh parsley, to garnish

■

1 Cut the veal into pencil-thin strips. Melt the butter in a frying pan and add the veal. Fry over high heat for 2–3 minutes, stirring constantly until lightly browned. Remove from the pan with a slotted spoon and set aside.

2 Add the stock to the pan and boil until reduced by half, stirring continuously.

3 Stir in the cream, mustard, lemon juice, browned veal, salt and pepper and simmer for 5 minutes, without boiling. Garnish with plenty of chopped parsley. Serve with buttered noodles and a tossed mixed salad.

■ TO COOK IN A MICROWAVE: Prepare the veal. Put the butter in a medium bowl and cook on HIGH for 1 minute until melted. Stir in the veal and stock. Cover and cook on HIGH for 12–15 minutes or until tender, stirring once. Stir in the cream, mustard, lemon juice, salt and pepper and cook on HIGH for a further 1–2 minutes until hot. Serve garnished with chopped parsley.

PORK ESCALOPES WITH JUNIPER

This dish is an ideal choice if you are inviting guests to dinner but haven't much time to prepare and cook beforehand.

■

SERVES 4

450 g (1 lb) pork fillet (tenderloin)

seasoned flour

about 25 g (1 oz) butter

5 tablespoons dry white wine

4 juniper berries, lightly crushed

150 ml (¼ pint) double cream

salt and pepper

chopped fresh parsley, to garnish

■

1 Cut the pork into 5 mm (¼ inch) slices. Beat out into thin slices between two sheets of dampened greaseproof paper, using a wooden rolling pin. Dip the pork escalopes in the seasoned flour and shake off any excess.

2 Heat the butter in a large frying pan and fry the escalopes briskly for 2 minutes on each side. Remove and keep warm.

3 Add the wine and junipers to the pan and boil rapidly, stirring in any sediment, until reduced by half. Pour in the cream, season and boil rapidly for 1 minute, stirring.

4 Pour over the escalopes, garnish and serve immediately.

■ TO COOK IN A MICROWAVE: Complete steps 1 and 2. Heat a large browning dish on HIGH for 5–8 minutes or according to manufacturer's instructions, adding 1 tablespoon oil instead of the butter for the last 15 seconds. Without removing the dish from the oven, add the pork and cook on HIGH for 2–3 minutes or until lightly browned on one side. Turn the pork over and cook on HIGH for a further 2–3 minutes or until the second side is brown. Remove from the dish. Add the wine and junipers to the dish, stirring in any sediment. Cook on HIGH for about 3–4 minutes until reduced by half. Add the cream and season. Cook on HIGH for 2 minutes until boiling. Pour over the escalopes and garnish.

LEMON AND PORK PATTIES

Beef used to be the only meat you could buy minced. Today, freshly minced pork and lamb and veal are all available.

∎

SERVES 4
1 small lemon
450 g (1 lb) lean minced pork
salt and pepper
butter
fresh sage
chicken stock
chopped fresh parsley
1–2 tablespoons single cream

∎

1 Grate the lemon rind into the mince, work in salt and lots of pepper. Divide into 8 and pat out into thin discs.
2 Melt butter to glaze a large frying pan and add a few sage leaves. Add half the patties and cook for 3 minutes each side until golden. Transfer to a warm serving dish. Cook the remainder.
3 Add a good squeeze of lemon juice and a little stock into the pan, stirring to lift the sediment at the bottom. Bubble down for a few minutes. Remove from the heat. Add lots of parsley and the cream. Pour over the patties and serve hot with a salad.
∎ TO COOK IN A MICROWAVE: Make the patties as in step 1. Meanwhile, heat a large browning dish on HIGH for 5–8 minutes or according to manufacturer's instructions, adding 1 tablespoon oil instead of the butter to the dish for the last 30 seconds. Add a few sage leaves and without removing the dish from the oven, add half the patties. Cook on HIGH for 2–3 minutes, then turn and reposition the patties and cook on HIGH for a further 2–3 minutes until cooked. Transfer the patties to a warmed serving dish. Cook the remaining patties in the same way. Add a good squeeze of lemon juice and a little stock, stirring in any sediment from the bottom of the dish. Cook on HIGH for 1 minute until boiling. Add lots of parsley and the cream. Pour over the patties and serve hot.

CHICKEN LIVERS IN GOLDEN BOXES

Puff pastry is now available in sheets. The beauty of these is that you don't have to roll out the pastry, simply take out the number of sheets you need from the box and leave to thaw. This will take about 20 minutes at room temperature.

■

SERVES 4
4 sheets of puff pastry, thawed
50 g (2 oz) butter or margarine
4 spring onions, trimmed and chopped
1 garlic clove
450 g (1 lb) chicken livers
splash of dry white wine
4 tablespoons single cream
2 tablespoons chopped fresh parsley
salt and pepper

■

1 Preheat the oven to 200°C (400°F) mark 6. Place the pastry sheets on dampened baking sheets and cut halfway through the pastry to form a lid, about 1 cm (½ inch) from the edge. Bake in the oven for 10–15 minutes until golden brown and well risen.

2 Melt the butter or margarine in a saucepan. Add the onions, crush in the garlic and cook for about 3 minutes until the onions are soft.

3 Add the chicken livers and cook for a further 5 minutes. Add the remaining ingredients and simmer for 2–3 minutes.

4 When the pastry boxes are cooked, transfer to warmed serving plates. Remove the lids and spoon in the chicken livers. Replace the lids at an angle and serve hot.

■ TO COOK IN A MICROWAVE: Complete step 1. Trim and chop the onions. Cut any whole chicken livers in half. Put the butter in a medium bowl and cook on HIGH for 1 minute until melted. Add the onions, crush in the garlic and cook on HIGH for 2 minutes until softened. Add the livers, cover and cook on HIGH for 3–4 minutes until the livers are cooked, stirring occasionally. Add the remaining ingredients; cook on HIGH for 1 minute. Complete step 4.

KIDNEYS IN SHERRY SAUCE

Sherry and wholegrain mustard combine well with kidneys. Citrus fruits also go well with offal. If liked, you can add some orange segments with the sherry.

■

SERVES 2
4 lamb's kidneys
1 small onion
2 rashers streaky bacon
small knob of butter
2 tablespoons flour
150 ml (¼ pint) chicken stock
1 tablespoon sherry
1 tablespoon wholegrain mustard
salt and pepper

■

1 Skin each kidney, cut in half lengthways, then snip out the core with scissors. Skin and finely chop the onion.

2 Using scissors, cut the bacon into pieces into a frying pan. Fry until the fat starts to run, then add the onion and cook until soft.

3 Add the butter and kidneys and cook until just firm. Stir in the flour, then gradually add the stock, stirring all the time. Add the sherry and simmer for 4–5 minutes. Do not boil, or the kidneys will toughen. Stir in the mustard, salt and pepper. Serve at once with rice and a green salad.

■ TO COOK IN A MICROWAVE: Complete step 1. Put the butter in a large bowl and cook on HIGH for 30 seconds until melted. Snip in the bacon, add the onion and cook on HIGH for 2–3 minutes until slightly softened. Stir in the flour and cook on HIGH for 1 minute. Gradually stir in the stock and sherry and cook on HIGH for 2–3 minutes until boiling and thickened, stirring occasionally. Add the kidneys and cook on HIGH for a further 4–5 minutes until the kidneys are tender, stirring occasionally. Stir in the mustard, salt and pepper and serve hot.

FISH FRITTO

Children like these as small fingers of fish are more appealing
to them than whole fillets of fried fish.

∎

SERVES 2

50 g (2 oz) self-raising white flour

2 large pinches of bicarbonate of soda

pinch of salt

225 g (8 oz) skinned haddock or halibut fillets

vegetable oil, for deep frying

∎

1 Sift the flour, bicarbonate of soda and salt into a bowl and
gradually add 125 ml (¼ pint) water, stirring all the time to make a
smooth, fairly thick batter. Whisk if necessary.
2 Remove any remaining bones from the fish and cut it into strips
the size of a little finger.
3 Heat the oil in a deep fat fryer to 180°C (350°F). Dip 6–8 pieces of
fish into the batter, drain off the excess and deep fry until golden.
Drain well while frying the remaining fish in the same way. Serve
hot in cones of greaseproof paper.

CRISPY BAKED FISH

Fillets of plaice or sole are particularly suitable for this dish, though any other fish fillets will do. Remember to choose thin fillets to speed up the cooking time.

■

SERVES 2
225 g (8 oz) thin fish fillets, skinned
vegetable oil
50 g (2 oz) dried breadcrumbs
salt and pepper

■

1 Wash and dry the fish and cut any large pieces in half. Dip into the oil, then coat with crumbs.
2 Arrange in a single layer in an oiled shallow dish and season with salt and pepper.
3 Bake at 200°C (400°F) mark 6 for 12–15 minutes without turning or basting. Serve with baked tomatoes and a fresh or frozen green vegetable such as peas or French beans.

Smoked Mackerel and
New Potato Salad

In this salad the potatoes are tossed in the dressing whilst still warm, so enabling them to absorb the flavour of the dressing more readily. Serve as a light lunch or supper dish.

■

SERVES 2
350 g (12 oz) very small new potatoes
salt
225 g (8 oz) smoked mackerel fillets
1 small onion
chopped fresh parsley
4 tablespoons French dressing

■

1 Cook the potatoes in boiling salted water for 10–15 minutes until tender.

2 Meanwhile, skin and flake the mackerel, removing any remaining bones. Skin and very finely chop the onion.

3 Drain the cooked potatoes and put in a serving dish. Pour over the dressing while they are still warm and toss together.

4 Stir in the mackerel and onion and sprinkle with chopped parsley. Serve while still warm, with a crisp green salad.

■ TO COOK IN A MICROWAVE: Cut any large potatoes in half. Put the potatoes in a large bowl with 4 tablespoons water. Cover and cook on HIGH for 6–8 minutes until tender, stirring occasionally. Complete the recipe.

PRAWN AND BACON BROCHETTES

WITH GARLIC BUTTER

Prawns and bacon combine beautifully. Served with a dish of rice, these brochettes make a delicious light lunch or supper at any time of the year. In the summer you can barbecue them instead of grilling them.

■

SERVES 2
40 g (1½ oz) butter
1 garlic clove
1 tablespoon chopped fresh parsley
1 teaspoon lemon juice
salt and pepper
6 rashers rindless streaky bacon
225 g (8 oz) cooked peeled prawns

■

1 Put the butter in a saucepan, crush in the garlic and heat until the butter has melted. Stir in the parsley, lemon juice, salt and pepper.
2 Using the back of a knife, stretch the bacon rashers, then cut in half widthways. Thread the bacon and prawns on to 6 skewers, winding the bacon under and over the prawns.
3 Dip the kebabs in the garlic butter, then arrange on a grill pan and grill for about 10 minutes until the prawns are cooked and the bacon crisp, turning several times during cooking.
4 Gently heat the remaining garlic butter and serve 3 kebabs each with the garlic butter poured over. Accompany with rice.
■ TO COOK IN A MICROWAVE: Put the butter and garlic in a shallow rectangular dish and cook on HIGH for 1 minute until the butter has melted. Complete steps 1 and 2. Thread the prawns and bacon on to wooden skewers. Dip in the garlic butter and arrange in a single layer in a dish. Cover with kitchen paper and cook on HIGH for 4–5 minutes until cooked, turning once.

YOU CAN MAKE THIS FOR MOTHER
WHEN SHE COMES OVER!!!

CHILLI MEDITERRANEAN PRAWNS

Don't overcook these juicy prawns or they will become tough and rubbery.

■

SERVES 1

3–4 uncooked Mediterranean prawns

2 tomatoes

1 medium fresh chilli

1 tablespoon olive oil

1 garlic clove

Tabasco

salt and pepper

■

1 Peel off the prawn shells. Skin and roughly chop the tomatoes. Remove the seeds and finely chop the chilli.
2 Heat the oil in a small frying pan. Add the prawns and cook, stirring, over a high heat for about 5 minutes.
3 Add the crushed garlic, tomatoes, chopped chilli, few drops of Tabasco, salt and pepper.
4 Cover and cook gently for a further 5 minutes or until the prawns are tender and the tomatoes reduced to a pulp. Serve with boiled rice and a green salad.

SCALLOPS WITH SAFFRON SAUCE

This not only tastes delicious, but the white scallops look very pretty with their yellow sauce.

■

SERVES 2
large pinch of saffron strands
4 tablespoons dry white wine
6 large shelled scallops
large knob of butter
1 small onion, skinned and finely chopped
4 tablespoons vegetable stock
4 tablespoons double cream
salt and pepper

■

1 Soak the saffron strands in a little of the wine. Meanwhile, if necessary, remove and discard the tough white 'muscle' from each scallop. Separate the corals from the scallops and set aside. Slice the white part across into 2 discs.

2 Heat the butter in a frying pan and fry the onion until soft. Add the scallops and cook for 1 minute. Add the corals and cook for a minute. Remove the scallops and arrange on 2 warmed plates.

3 Stir the remaining wine and stock into the pan and boil rapidly until reduced by half, stirring continuously. Stir in the cream, saffron, salt and pepper. Bring back to the boil and boil for 1–2 minutes until slightly thickened then spoon around the scallops.

■ TO COOK IN A MICROWAVE: Complete step 1. Put the butter in a medium bowl and cook on HIGH for 30 seconds until melted. Add the onion and cook on HIGH for 4–5 minutes until softened. Add the scallops and cook on HIGH for 2 minutes until they are just opaque. Add the corals and cook on HIGH for a further minute until tender. Remove the scallops from the bowl. Stir in the remaining wine and stock and cook on HIGH for 4–5 minutes until boiling and reduced by half. Stir in the cream, dissolved saffron, salt and pepper and cook on HIGH for 2 minutes until slightly thickened. Complete the recipe.

CAULIFLOWER AND BROCCOLI STILTONS

Cauliflower cheese is an old faithful when you want to prepare a quick meal. This is an adaptation of that old favourite.

■

SERVES 2

1 small cauliflower

175 g (6 oz) broccoli

a large knob of butter or margarine

2 tablespoons flour

300 ml (½ pint) milk

75 g (3 oz) Stilton cheese

broken walnuts

■

1 Cut the cauliflower and broccoli into florets and slice their stalks. Cook in boiling water for 5 minutes until just tender.

2 Meanwhile, put the butter, flour and milk in a saucepan, slowly bring to the boil, whisking continuously, until the sauce thickens. Simmer for 1–2 minutes.

3 Crumble in the cheese, give a stir and heat to serving temperature. Pour over the drained vegetables, then scatter with the nuts before serving.

■ TO COOK IN A MICROWAVE: Prepare the vegetables and put in a large shallow dish with 2 tablespoons water. Cover and cook on HIGH for 7–8 minutes until tender. Put the butter, flour and milk in a medium bowl and stir together. Cook on HIGH for 3½–4½ minutes until the sauce has boiled and thickened, whisking every minute. Crumble in the cheese and stir well. Pour over the drained vegetables, then scatter with the nuts before serving.

SPAGHETTI ALLA CARBONARA

Lovers of pasta can make this tasty dish in no time at all. The flavour is much improved by the use of fresh Parmesan cheese.

■

SERVES 4
450 g (1 lb) spaghetti
salt and pepper
1 tablespoon olive or vegetable oil
225 g (8 oz) bacon, cut into thin strips
1 small onion, skinned and finely chopped
1 garlic clove, skinned and finely chopped
4 eggs
4 tablespoons freshly grated Parmesan cheese, plus extra for serving
4 tablespoons single cream
25 g (1 oz) butter

■

1 Cook the spaghetti in a large saucepan of boiling salted water for about 8 minutes or until just tender.

2 Meanwhile, heat the oil in a frying pan, add the bacon, onion and garlic and fry for 5–7 minutes until softened. Beat the eggs in a bowl with the cheese, cream, salt and pepper.

3 Drain the pasta well, return to the hot saucepan and toss with the butter. Pour in the egg mixture and mix well.

4 Stir in the bacon mixture with its juices. Serve with the cheese.

■ TO COOK IN A MICROWAVE: Put the spaghetti in a large bowl and pour over about 1.7 litres (3 pints) boiling water. Stir, cover and cook on HIGH for 6–8 minutes until just tender. Leave to stand, covered. Do not drain. Meanwhile, prepare the bacon, onion and garlic. Put the oil in a medium bowl and cook on HIGH for 30 seconds until hot. Add the bacon, onion and garlic and cook on HIGH for 4–5 minutes until softened. Meanwhile, beat the eggs in a bowl with the cheese, cream, salt and pepper. Drain the pasta and return to the bowl. Toss in the butter, bacon mixture and egg mixture. Cook on HIGH for 1 minute, stirring once, until the egg is just set.

RASPBERRY BAKED ALASKA

Keep the ice cream in the freezer until the last moment so that it's as firm as possible before you bake it. This dessert looks impressive but is actually quite quick and simple.

∎

SERVES 4–6

15cm (6 inch) bought sponge flan case

300 g (11 oz) can raspberries in fruit juice

2 tablespoons dark rum (optional)

3 egg whites

50 g (2 oz) caster sugar

485 ml (17 fl oz) block vanilla ice cream

∎

1 Place the flan case on an ovenproof plate. Drain the raspberries, reserving the juice. Spoon the rum and 3 tablespoons of the reserved juice over the flan case. (Add more juice if omitting the rum.) Spoon in the raspberries.
2 Whisk the egg whites until stiff but not dry, add the sugar and whisk again until they regain their former stiffness.
3 Place the vanilla ice cream in the centre of the flan case, cutting to fit into the flan. Cover completely with the meringue.
4 Bake straight away at 230°C (450°F) mark 8 for 2–3 minutes only. The meringue should be nicely tinged with brown. Serve at once before the ice cream begins to melt.

Mango Fool

Ripe mangoes have a yellow or orange skin and give' if gently squeezed. As an alternative, you can use fresh peaches or nectarines in this recipe.

■

SERVES 2–4 depending on size of mango
1 ripe mango
3 teaspoons orange liqueur
1–2 tablespoons Greek strained yogurt
1 small orange

■

1 Slice the mango into quarters lengthwise through to the stone. With a small knife, remove flesh from around the stone, then scoop away the rest from the skin – do this over a bowl with a teaspoon.
2 Put the flesh and orange liqueur into a food processor or blender and work to form a purée. Fold in the yogurt.
3 Peel and slice the orange. Reserve a few slices to decorate and roughly chop the remaining slices. Divide between individual serving dishes and pour in the mango purée. Decorate with the reserved orange slices.

AMARETTI APRICOT COMPOTE

Choose the no-soak apricots available in most large supermarkets for this recipe. The very dried varieties will not soften in the time allowed.

∎

SERVES 4

220 g (7 oz) no-soak dried apricots

1 tablespoon Amaretto di Saronno (almond liqueur)

flaked almonds

∎

1 Put the apricots in a small saucepan with 300 ml (½ pint) water. Bring to the boil, cover and simmer for about 12 minutes until tender.
2 Using a slotted spoon, place the apricots in a serving dish. Bubble down the cooking liquor until it has reduced by half.
3 Stir in the liqueur, pour the juices over the apricots and decorate with a few toasted flaked almonds. Serve warm.
∎ TO COOK IN A MICROWAVE: Put the apricots in a medium bowl with 300 ml (½ pint) water. Cover and cook on HIGH for 5 minutes until boiling and the apricots are plump. Using a slotted spoon, place the apricots in a serving dish. Cook the cooking liquor on HIGH for 5–6 minutes until reduced by half, then complete the recipe.

DROP SCONES

Made from store cupboard ingredients, Drop Scones are ideal for an impromptu tea party. Serve them with butter and jam or honey.

■

MAKES 16–18
150 g (5 oz) self-raising flour
pinch of salt
1 tablespoon caster sugar
1 egg
1 tablespoon vegetable oil, plus extra for greasing
150 ml (¼ pint) milk

■

1 Sift the flour and salt into a bowl. Add the sugar. Beat the egg and add with the oil and milk. Stir with a wooden spoon to combine to a thick batter.
2 Grease a griddle or heavy frying pan with a little oil and place over medium heat until hot.
3 Drop spoonfuls of the mixture on to the pan, keeping them well apart to allow for spreading.
4 Cook over medium heat for 2–3 minutes until bubbles rise and burst all over the surface and the undersides are golden brown. Turn over with a palette knife and cook for 2–3 minutes on the other side.
5 Transfer the cooked scones to a clean tea-towel and fold the cloth over to enclose them while making the remaining scones. Serve hot, as soon as all the scones are made.

CHAPTER 4

20 – 30 MINUTES

COCOTTE EGGS WITH COURGETTES

Serve as a light lunch or supper dish with fingers of wholemeal or granary (wholegrain) toast. As an alternative to the courgettes in this recipe, you can use mushrooms.

■

SERVES 2

1 medium courgette

1 tablespoon vegetable oil

2 tablespoons crème fraîche

2 eggs

150 ml (¼ pint) milk

pinch of ground cumin

salt and pepper

■

1 Slice the courgette, then cook in the oil until softened. Spoon into 2 cocottes or individual soufflé dishes. Whisk the remaining ingredients together – not too frothy – and pour into the dishes.
2 Stand the dishes in a roasting tin with hot water to come halfway up the sides of the dishes. Cook at 150°C (300°F) mark 2 for about 20 minutes until set.

OPPOSITE: SPEEDY PAN PIZZA

page 84

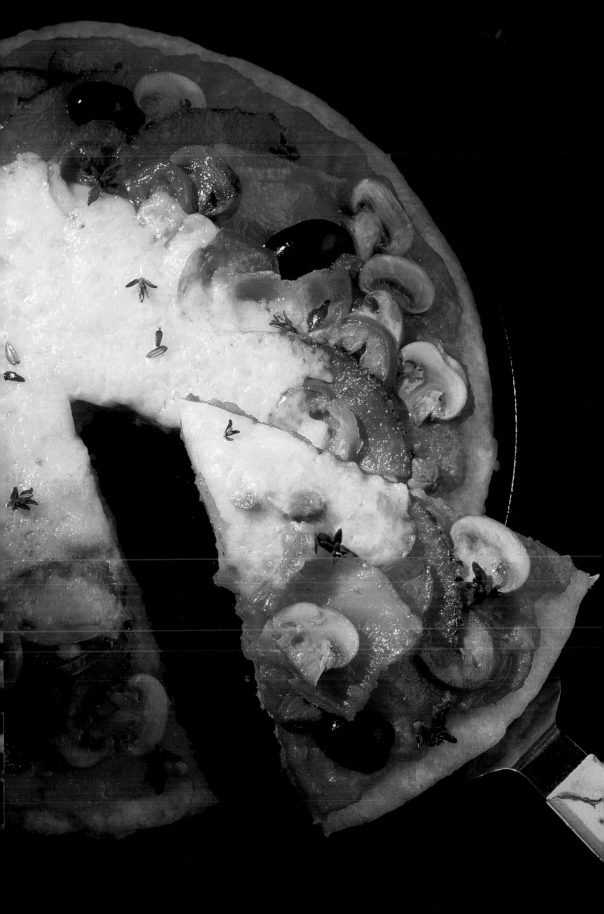

ROSEMARY WALNUTS

Friends popping round for a pre-dinner drink? If you want to offer them something more than the traditional packet of peanuts, warm roasted walnuts look as though you've tried even though they are no effort and the result is quite delicious!

∎

MAKES 225 g (8 oz)
large knob of butter
1 tablespoon olive oil
225 g (8 oz) walnut halves
2 teaspoons dried or 3 tablespoons finely chopped fresh rosemary
1 teaspoon paprika
1 teaspoon salt

∎

1 Preheat the oven to 170°C (325°F) mark 4. Put the butter and oil in a large roasting tin and melt in the oven.
2 Add the nuts to the pan and stir in the butter mixture until evenly coated, then spread them out in a single layer. Scatter the rosemary, paprika and salt over the nuts.
3 Bake in the oven for 20-25 minutes until the nuts are golden brown, shaking and turning the nuts several times during cooking. Drain on kitchen paper and serve warm.

OPPOSITE: SMOKED SALMON AND TARAMASALATA MOUSSE

page 100

SESAME PRAWN TOASTS

I don't know anyone who needs an excuse to eat these! If you do, serve them as a starter, otherwise make them for a snack any time of day.

■

MAKES 18
1 spring onion
1 cm (½ inch) piece of fresh root ginger
225 g (8 oz) cooked peeled prawns
1 small egg white
1 tablespoon cornflour
large pinch of salt
6 thin slices of white bread
75 g (3 oz) sesame seeds
vegetable oil, for deep frying

■

1 Trim and finely chop the spring onion. Peel the ginger.
2 Put the ginger in a food processor and work until finely chopped. Add the prawns and chop finely. Add the onions, egg white, cornflour and salt and work to form a smooth paste.
3 Cut the crusts off the bread. Spread the prawn paste evenly on each slice.
4 Spread the sesame seeds on a plate and press the prawn side of each bread slice into the sesame seeds to coat well.
5 Heat the oil in a deep-fat frier to 180°C (350°F). Slide 2 prawn slices at a time into the hot oil. Deep fry for 3 minutes, turning once, until golden brown. Remove with a slotted spoon and drain on kitchen paper. Cook the remaining prawn toasts in the same way. Cut each slice of bread into 3 fingers and serve with sweet chilli or hoisin sauce to dip.

SPICY NUT BURGERS

These are absolutely delicious for a light lunch or supper dish and are ideal for vegetarians.

■

SERVES 2
6 tablespoons vegetable oil
1 medium onion, skinned and finely chopped
1 medium carrot, peeled and grated
½ teaspoon cumin seeds
¼ teaspoon ground coriander
1 garlic clove
100 g (4 oz) finely chopped mixed nuts
50 g (2 oz) brown breadcrumbs
50 g (2 oz) Cheddar cheese
salt and pepper
1 egg

■

1 Heat 2 tablespoons of the oil in a saucepan and add the onion, carrot, cumin and coriander. Crush in the garlic and fry for 5 minutes until the onion is soft. Turn into a bowl, add the nuts and breadcrumbs and grate in the cheese. Season and stir well to mix. Beat in the egg to bind the mixture together. Divide into 6 and shape into burgers.

2 Heat the remaining oil in a frying pan, add the burgers and fry for 3–4 minutes on each side until golden brown. Drain on absorbent kitchen paper and serve.

■ TO COOK IN A MICROWAVE: Put 2 tablespoons of the oil, the onion, carrot, cumin, coriander and crushed garlic into a medium bowl. Cover and cook on HIGH for 5 minutes or until the vegetables have softened, stirring occasionally. Complete step 1. Heat a large browning dish on HIGH for 5–8 minutes or according to manufacturer's instructions. When the dish is hot, add only 2 tablespoons of the remaining oil and cook on HIGH for 30 seconds. Without removing the dish from the oven, put the burgers in the dish and cook on HIGH for 1½ minutes; turn over and cook on HIGH for a further 1 minute or until browned.

Speedy Pan Pizza

This pizza is quick to make because the base is made from scone dough instead of the traditional bread dough. It is then cooked in a frying pan instead of the oven. This is a basic pizza and you can vary the topping according to what you have and what your favourite ingredients are. Add on top of the tomatoes and before covering with cheese. Try sliced salami, sliced ham, fried chopped bacon, anchovy fillets, drained bottled mussels, drained capers or fried mushrooms.

■

SERVES 2
397 g (14 oz) can chopped tomatoes
175 g (6 oz) Cheddar cheese
225 g (8 oz) self-raising flour
salt and pepper
4 tablespoons vegetable oil
4 tablespoons tomato purée
a few black olives
chopped fresh herbs

■

1 Drain and chop the tomatoes. Grate the cheese.
2 Put the flour in a bowl and season with salt and pepper. Make a well in the centre and pour in 2 tablespoons of the oil and 6 tablespoons of water. Mix to a soft dough, adding more water if necessary. Roll out to a circle to fit a medium frying pan.
3 Heat half the remaining oil in the pan. Add the dough and fry gently for about 5 minutes until the base is lightly browned.
4 Turn the dough out on to a plate and flip over. Heat the remaining oil in the pan, then slide the dough back into the pan, browned side uppermost.
5 Spread with the tomato purée, then top with the tomatoes. Sprinkle over the cheese and black olives.
6 Cook for a further 5 minutes until the underside is cooked, then slide the pan under a preheated grill. Cook for 3–4 minutes until the cheese melts. Serve hot, sprinkled with chopped herbs.

MIXED VEGETABLE CASSEROLE

The broccoli florets can be used whole in the following recipe, but by boiling and puréeing them instead you end up with delicious thickened juices for the casserole. This is an ideal dish for vegetarians, but if you want to add some meat you can add some chopped ham or smoked sausage.

■

SERVES 2
225 g (8 oz) broccoli
1 small cauliflower
1 medium onion
1 teaspoon coriander seeds
2 tablespoons vegetable oil
1 garlic clove
425 g (15 oz) can butter beans
150 ml (6 fl oz) chicken stock
salt and pepper
6 tablespoons wholemeal breadcrumbs
100 g (4 oz) smoked cheese

■

1 Divide the broccoli into florets and cook in boiling water until tender. Meanwhile, divide the cauliflower into florets. Skin and chop the onion. Crush the coriander seeds.
2 Drain the cooked broccoli, put in to a food processor and work to form a purée.
3 Heat the oil in a small flameproof casserole dish. Add the cauliflower florets, onion, coriander seeds and crush in the garlic. Cook, stirring, for 3–4 minutes.
4 Mix in the drained butter beans, stock, puréed broccoli, salt and pepper. Simmer, covered, for about 10 minutes until the cauliflower is tender.
5 Sprinkle the breadcrumbs and grate the cheese over the vegetables and flash under a hot grill. Serve with thick slices of wholemeal bread.

Italian Chicken with Rosemary and Vinegar

Serve this simple Italian dish as a family meal.

■

SERVES 4
large sprig of fresh rosemary
2 tablespoons white wine vinegar
salt and pepper
4 chicken breasts, with skins on
2 tablespoons olive oil

■

1 Finely chop the rosemary and put in a bowl with the vinegar, 1 tablespoon water, salt and pepper. Leave to infuse while cooking the chicken.

2 Season the chicken pieces with salt and pepper. Heat the oil in a large frying pan and fry the chicken for about 30 minutes until tender and golden brown. Turn the chicken over occasionally during cooking.

3 Lower the heat. When the fat has stopped sizzling, pour over the vinegar infusion. Bring to the boil and boil rapidly for 2–3 minutes to reduce the liquid, then serve at once. Accompany with boiled potatoes and Italian style courgettes (see page 13) or tomatoes.

■ TO COOK IN A MICROWAVE: Complete step 1. Heat a large browning dish on HIGH for 5–8 minutes or according to manufacturer's instructions, adding the oil for the last 15 seconds. Without removing the dish from the oven, quickly place the chicken pieces, skin side down, in the hot fat. Cook on HIGH for 8–10 minutes, turning the chicken over halfway during cooking. Pour over the vinegar infusion and cook on HIGH for 2 minutes until boiling. Serve hot.

CHICKEN IN ORANGE SAUCE

Citrus fruits combine beautifully with chicken. In this case, oranges, tarragon and a few spoonfuls of dry white wine, which is hardly extravagant, are reduced to a delicious sauce.

∎

SERVES 4
4 chicken breast fillets, skinned
plain flour
salt
large pinch of paprika
2 medium oranges
4 tablespoons dry white wine
large pinch of dried or 1 tablespoon chopped fresh tarragon
6 tablespoons double cream
vegetable oil, for shallow frying
large knob of butter

∎

1 Slash the fillets with a knife and coat in flour, seasoned with salt and paprika. Using a zester, pare the rind of the oranges into shreds then squeeze out the juice of the oranges into a small pan.
2 Heat the orange juice, wine, tarragon and half of the orange shreds and boil to reduce by half.
3 Meanwhile, fry the chicken fillets in the oil and butter for 3–4 minutes each side.
4 Add the cream and a pinch of salt to the sauce and heat gently. Serve the chicken fillets with the orange sauce poured over. Garnish with the reserved orange shreds. Accompany with boiled potatoes and a green vegetable such as courgettes, French beans or broccoli.

MINI CHICKEN AND PINE NUT KOFTAS

Koftas are meatballs originating from the Middle East. There are numerous recipes. They can be made from beef, lamb, veal or chicken, and they can be large or small, grilled, fried, steamed or poached and seasoned with a variety of spices. These chicken koftas have pine nuts added but there is no reason why you cannot use pistachios or almonds instead.

∎

SERVES 4

2 small, thin slices of white bread

4 chicken breast fillets, skinned

50 g (2 oz) pine nuts

large handful of chopped fresh parsley

small pinch of ground cinnamon

pinch of paprika

1 egg

salt and pepper

flour, for dusting

oil, for shallow frying

∎

1 Put the bread in a food processor or blender and work to form breadcrumbs. Add the chicken and work until finely minced.
2 Add the pine nuts, parsley, cinnamon, paprika, egg, salt and pepper and mix very thoroughly until the mixture is smooth.
3 With wet hands, shape the mixture evenly into about 20 small balls, about the size of a walnut. Lightly dust with flour.
4 Heat about 1 cm (½ inch) oil in a large frying pan, then add the meatballs and cook for about 10 minutes, turning frequently, until golden brown. Drain on absorbent kitchen paper. Serve with rice or in pockets of warm pitta (Lebanese) bread, together with a salad and lemon wedges. They can also be served with a tomato sauce.

LAMB CHOPS WITH MINT AND TAHINI

Fried or grilled lamb chops have long been a favourite with cooks in a hurry. Here, in an interesting variation on an old theme, they are served with a mint and tahini sauce. Tahini is a paste of sesame seeds sold in jars at supermarkets and delicatessens.

■

SERVES 4
2 tablespoons vegetable oil
large knob of butter or margarine
4 lamb chump chops
1 garlic clove
2 tablespoons chopped fresh mint, plus sprigs, to garnish
1 tablespoon tahini
1 teaspoon lemon juice
salt and pepper

■

1 Heat the oil and butter together in a frying pan. Add the chops and cook for 15–20 minutes, turning several times. Transfer to warmed serving plates.

2 Crush the garlic into the pan and add the mint. Stir in the tahini, lemon juice, salt and pepper, stirring to loosen any sediment at the bottom of the pan. Cook for 1 minute until hot.

3 Spoon the sauce over the chops and serve garnished with mint sprigs. Accompany with boiled potatoes and a green vegetable.

■ TO COOK IN A MICROWAVE: Heat a large browning dish on HIGH for 5–8 minutes or according to manufacturer's instructions. Add the oil and butter. Then, without removing the dish from the cooker, add the lamb and cook on HIGH for 2 minutes. Turn the meat over and cook on HIGH for a further 6–8 minutes or until just cooked. Transfer to warmed serving plates. Crush the garlic into the dish and add the mint, tahini, lemon juice, salt and pepper, stirring to loosen any sediment at the bottom of the dish. Microwave on HIGH for 1 minute, stirring once. Spoon the sauce over the chops and serve garnished with mint sprigs.

LAMB AND OLIVE PILAFF

This pilaff is simple to cook and is a complete meal in itself.

■

SERVES 2
225 g (8 oz) lamb neck fillet or boneless leg steaks
1 large onion
6 green olives
vegetable oil
100 g (4 oz) long-grain white rice
200 ml (7 fl oz) lamb or chicken stock
rosemary sprigs
salt and pepper
100 g (4 oz) frozen peas

■

1 Cut the lamb into bite-sized pieces. Slice the onion and halve the olives.
2 Heat a little oil in a frying pan and fry the lamb and onion until browned. Stir in the rice, stock, few rosemary sprigs, olives, salt and pepper.
3 Bring to the boil, cover and simmer for 10 minutes. Stir in the peas and cook for a further 5 minutes or until the rice is tender and the stock absorbed.

Lamb and Mint Meatballs

Minced lamb is almost as easily available as minced beef now but if it is not available in your area you can use minced beef and parsley instead. Here, lamb meatballs are served hot as a main course but you can also make them smaller and serve them cold as an appetiser.

■

SERVES 4

1 medium onion

large handful of fresh mint leaves

450 g (1 lb) lean minced lamb

1 egg

salt and pepper

1 garlic clove

flour, for coating

vegetable oil, for frying

■

1 Skin and finely chop the onion. Finely chop the mint.
2 In a large bowl, put the lamb, onion, mint, egg, salt and pepper. Crush in the garlic. Beat together until well mixed. With floured hands, form the mixture into about 12 even sized balls.
3 Heat enough oil in a frying pan to cover the base, then cook the meatballs for 10–15 minutes, turning frequently, until golden brown. Drain on absorbent kitchen paper and serve hot or cold with boiled rice and a tomato sauce.
■ TO COOK IN A MICROWAVE: Complete steps 1 and 2. Arrange the meatballs in a single layer in a shallow dish. Without adding any oil, cook on HIGH for 6–8 minutes until cooked, rearranging once during cooking.

ORANGE-GLAZED GAMMON STEAKS

For everyday family meals, gammon steaks and bacon chops
are a good buy as they cook so quickly.

■

SERVES 4
1 tablespoon cornflour
1 tablespoon lemon juice
8 tablespoons orange juice
1 tablespoon soy sauce
1 tablespoon honey
large pinch of mustard powder
small pinch of ground ginger
salt and pepper
4 gammon steaks or bacon chops

■

1 Blend the cornflour with the lemon juice, then stir in all the
remaining ingredients except the gammon steaks. Put into a
saucepan, bring to the boil, stirring all the time, until the mixture
thickens.
2 Arrange the gammon steaks or bacon chops on a grill pan and
brush half of the glaze on one side. Grill under a medium heat for
15 minutes, until cooked and brown. Turn the meat several times
during cooking, brushing with the remaining glaze. Serve hot,
accompanied by boiled potatoes and stir-fried courgette shreds
(see page 12).
■ TO COOK IN A MICROWAVE: The glaze can be prepared in a
microwave. Complete step 1, putting the mixture into a medium
bowl. Cook on HIGH for 2–3 minutes until boiling and thickened,
whisking every minute.

LIVER STROGANOFF

This is a variation on the better known Beef Stroganoff, one of the classic dishes of quick cuisine. The dish was apparently named after the Russian Count Stroganoff, though nobody knows exactly when or why.

■

SERVES 4
4 slices of lamb's liver
1 medium onion
225 g (8 oz) button mushrooms
25 g (1 oz) butter or margarine
2 teaspoons Dijon mustard
2 tablespoons brandy (optional)
salt and pepper
150 ml (¼ pint) soured cream

■

1 Slice the liver into thin strips. Thinly slice the onion and mushrooms. Melt the butter in a large frying pan, add the liver and fry for about 5 minutes, stirring constantly so that the strips become evenly and lightly coloured. Remove with a slotted spoon and set aside.

2 Add the sliced onion to the pan and fry for about 5 minutes until soft. Remove the onion from the pan with a slotted spoon and add to the liver.

3 Add the mushrooms to the pan, increase the heat and toss until the juices run. Remove and add to the liver and onions.

4 Stir the mustard into the pan juices, then the brandy if using. Stir over high heat, scraping up the sediment from the base of the pan.

5 Return the liver, onion and mushrooms to the pan and stir to combine with the juices. Add salt and pepper, then remove from the heat.

6 Stir the soured cream vigorously, then stir about half into the stroganoff. Serve the stroganoff with the remaining soured cream drizzled over the top. Accompany with noodles.

CUCUMBER TROUT

To save time, buy the trout already cleaned.

■

SERVES 2
7.5 cm (3 inch) piece of cucumber
2–3 spring onions
2 tablespoons ground hazelnuts
3 tablespoons fresh brown breadcrumbs
salt and pepper
2 medium pink trout, cleaned
melted butter
lemon juice

■

1 Grate the cucumber coarsely into a bowl. Slice the spring onions and add to the bowl with the nuts, breadcrumbs, salt and pepper.
2 Stuff the trout with this mixture. Place on a grill rack, brush all over with melted butter and splash with lemon juice. Cook under a medium/high grill for 15–20 minutes, turning once. Be careful not to overbrown. Serve with boiled new potatoes and a green vegetable or mushrooms.
■ TO COOK IN A MICROWAVE: Stuff the trout with the prepared mixture. Place the trout, side by side, in a large dish. Cover and cook on HIGH for 5–7 minutes until tender.

SMOKED HADDOCK KEDGEREE

Kedgeree is often associated with brunch. The weekend is probably the only time that you would serve brunch so enjoy this kedgeree with smoked haddock for an evening meal if brunch is not something that fits into your lifestyle!

■

SERVES 4
225 g (8 oz) long-grain rice
salt and pepper
450 g (1 lb) smoked haddock fillets
2 eggs
50 g (2 oz) butter or margarine
chopped fresh parsley, to garnish

■

1 Cook the rice, uncovered, in a large saucepan of fast-boiling salted water for about 12 minutes until tender.

2 Meanwhile, put the haddock in a frying pan with just enough water to cover. Bring to simmering point, then simmer for 10–15 minutes until tender. Cook the eggs in a small saucepan of boiling water for 10 minutes.

3 Drain the cooked rice. Drain, skin and flake the fish, discarding the bones. Drain the eggs, run under cold water and remove the shells. Roughly chop the hard-boiled eggs.

4 Melt the butter in the large saucepan, add the rice, fish, eggs, salt and pepper and stir over a medium heat for about 5 minutes until hot. Serve garnished with chopped parsley.

■ TO COOK IN A MICROWAVE: Put the rice and 600 ml (1 pint) boiling water in a large bowl. Stir once, then cover and cook on HIGH for 12 minutes. Leave to stand, covered. Meanwhile, put the haddock in a large dish with 2 tablespoons water, cover and cook on HIGH for 4–5 minutes, until tender. Complete steps 2 and 3, cooking the eggs conventionally. Put the butter in a large bowl and cook on HIGH for 1 minute until melted. Add the rice, fish, eggs, salt and pepper and cook on HIGH for 2–3 minutes until hot. Serve garnished with chopped parsley.

SALMON EN PAPILLOTE

Cooking fish en papillote ensures that all the flavour and juices are retained inside a greaseproof paper parcel. This dish is also very easy to prepare, whether you use salmon or another firm fish such as brill, cod or haddock. Salmon is delicious served with Hollandaise Sauce which you can make while the fish is cooking. Follow the recipe on page 124.

■

SERVES 2

2 salmon fillets, each weighing 150 g (5 oz)

butter

salt and pepper

100 g (4 oz) cooked peeled prawns

lemon juice

■

1 Place the salmon fillets on squares of buttered greaseproof paper and season with salt and pepper.

2 Spoon the prawns over the fish and dot with butter. Squeeze lemon juice over each.

3 Fold the paper edges tightly to make a plump parcel. Place the parcels on a baking tray and bake at 180°C (350°F) mark 4 for 15-20 minutes until the fish is tender. Serve with Hollandaise Sauce, if liked (see page 124). Accompany with mange-tout and new boiled potatoes.

■ TO COOK IN A MICROWAVE: Place the prepared parcels on an ovenproof plate and microwave on HIGH for 3½–4 minutes until the fish is tender.

OPPOSITE: LAMB FILLET WITH CREAMY LEEK SAUCE

page 103

FRUIT CHEESECAKE

This cheesecake is both quick to make and easy to assemble. As the cheese mixture is sufficiently firm to hold its shape, it requires neither gelatine to set it, nor baking time. The most difficult part is choosing your topping; almost any canned fruit, canned fruit pie filling or fresh fruit will do.

■

SERVES 6
175 g (6 oz) digestive biscuits
75 g (3 oz) butter
225 g (8 oz) cream cheese
4 tablespoons caster sugar
300 ml (½ pint) double cream
1 tablespoon lemon juice
400 g (14 oz) can of fruit, drained, or a can of pie filling or fresh fruit in season

■

1 Put the biscuits in a food processor and work until finely crushed. Melt the butter in a saucepan and stir in the crushed biscuits until well mixed.
2 Press the mixture into the base and sides of a 20 cm (8 inch) fluted flan case. Put in the refrigerator while preparing the filling.
3 Put the cheese in a bowl and beat until soft, then beat in the sugar. Pour in the cream and, using an electric whisk, whisk until thick. Do not overwhisk. Stir in the lemon juice.
4 Spoon the mixture into the flan case and level the surface. Refrigerate for about 10 minutes.
5 Spoon the can of fruit or pie filling over the top of the cheesecake or decorate with fresh fruit and serve.
■ TO COOK IN A MICROWAVE: The butter can be melted in a microwave. Cut it into cubes and put in a smal bowl. Cook on HIGH for 1½–2 minutes until melted.

OPPOSITE: CRANACHAN

page 109

KIWI FRUIT AND LEMON SYLLABUB

A very pretty dessert to serve when entertaining. It takes only 15 minutes to prepare, the rest of the time is for leaving it to chill. For a mid-week family dessert, bananas can be used instead of the kiwi fruit, natural yogurt can replace the cream and you can omit the wine.

■

SERVES 4
4 kiwi fruit
12 tiny ratafia biscuits or 8 macaroons
170 ml (6 fl oz) chilled whipping cream
5 tablespoons sweet white wine
3 tablespoons lemon curd

■

1 Peel the kiwi fruit. Slice enough to line 4 glass dishes. Chop the remaining fruit and combine with crushed ratafias in the base of the glasses.
2 Whisk the chilled cream, wine and lemon curd together until thick and floppy. Spoon into the glasses.
3 Chill for 15 minutes in the freezer or longer in the refrigerator before serving.

CHAPTER 5

30–45 MINUTES

Smoked Salmon and
Taramasalata Mousse

This looks pretty and tastes good, too. It makes a delicious starter when you are entertaining or you can serve it for a special light lunch with a green salad. Garnish with a spoonful of thick Greek yogurt sprinkled with lump fish roe or simply a twist of lemon and perhaps a black olive.

■

SERVES 4
125 g (4 oz) very thinly sliced smoked salmon
225 g (8 oz) taramasalata
225 g (8 oz) cream cheese
2 tablespoons lemon juice
a good pinch of cayenne

■

1 Lightly oil 4 ramekin dishes. Carefully line with the salmon, then finely chop any remaining pieces.

2 In a bowl, stir together the remaining ingredients and add the chopped salmon. Divide among the dishes. Chill in the refrigerator for 30 minutes. Serve turned out on individual plates. Garnish and accompany with French bread.

CHICKEN EN CROUTE

A packet of pastry in the freezer is always a useful standby. All
you have to do is remember to take it out in advance to thaw.
Here it is used with only two other ingredients for a quick
delicious meal.

■

SERVES 4

4 sheets of frozen puff pastry, thawed

4 chicken breast fillets, skinned

4 tablespoons mango chutney

■

1 Preheat the oven to 200°C (400°F) mark 6. On a lightly floured
work surface, roll out each sheet of pastry large enough to wrap
the chicken in.
2 Place a chicken breast in the centre of each pastry square, slash
each 3 times and spread the mango chutney evenly on top and
into the slashes.
3 Dampen the pastry edges, fold over to cover the chicken completely, sealing the edges well.
4 Place on a dampened baking sheet with the joins at the bottom
and bake for 25 minutes until golden brown. Serve with a salad or
green vegetable such as French beans or spinach.

TANDOORI CHICKEN

This is a speedy version of the Indian recipe, where the chicken is usually marinated in the spice mixture. It is also cooked in an oven and not a tandoor. In the summer you can cook the chicken on a barbecue. Although this recipe cuts corners, it still tastes good!

∎

SERVES 4–8
8 chicken drumsticks, thighs or breasts, skinned
2 tablespoons lemon juice
2 garlic cloves, skinned
2.5 cm (1 inch) piece of fresh root ginger
pinch of ground chilli
large pinch of ground cumin
150 ml (¼ pint) natural yogurt
1 teaspoon garam masala
1 tablespoon paprika
1 tablespoon tomato purée
1 teaspoon salt
1 tablespoon vegetable oil
lemon wedges, to garnish

∎

1 In a roasting tin, slash the skinned chicken all over and rub with the lemon juice. Put all the remaining ingredients, except the lemon wedges, in a food processor or blender and work to form a purée. Spoon over the chicken.
2 Roast in the oven at 200°C (400°F) mark 6 for 30–40 minutes until tender, basting occasionally during cooking. Garnish with lemon wedges and serve with a cucumber salad and rice.

LAMB FILLET WITH
CREAMY LEEK SAUCE

This is a delicious dish to serve when entertaining or as an
alternative to the traditional Sunday roast lunch.

■

SERVES 4
2 lamb fillets, total weight about 550 g (1¼ lb)
1 garlic clove
salt and pepper
2 fresh rosemary sprigs, plus extra to garnish
450 g (1 lb) leeks
150 ml (¼ pint) single cream
whole nutmeg

■

1 Put the lamb fillets in a roasting tin and crush the garlic on top.
Spread over the lamb, season with pepper and add the rosemary
sprigs. Roast at 180°C (350°F) mark 4 for 30 minutes until tender.
2 Meanwhile trim, slice and wash the leeks. Cook in boiling
salted water for 10 minutes until tender. Drain well and put in a
food processor or blender. Work until smooth.
3 Return to the saucepan and stir in the cream, a little grated
nutmeg, salt and pepper. Add any cooking juices from the
cooked lamb to the sauce. Stirring, gently reheat the sauce.
4 Slice the lamb and arrange on warm serving plates. Spoon a
little sauce over the lamb and serve the rest separately. Garnish
with rosemary sprigs.
■ TO COOK IN A MICROWAVE: Put the prepared leeks and 4 tablespoons water in a medium bowl. Cover and cook on HIGH for 10
minutes, stirring once. Drain well. Blend until smooth. Return to
the bowl and stir in the cream, a little grated nutmeg, salt and
pepper. Put the lamb on a rack. Crush the garlic on top, spread
over the lamb, season with pepper and add the rosemary sprigs.
Cook, uncovered, on HIGH for 3 minutes. Cover and cook on
MEDIUM for 15 minutes, rearranging twice, until cooked to your
liking. Add any cooking juices from the cooked lamb to the sauce.
Reheat the sauce on HIGH until hot. Meanwhile slice the lamb
and complete step 4.

PORK WITH CHILLI BEANS

Cooking dried beans from scratch takes a long time and the difference in the result is barely detectable from the ready-prepared canned variety, especially in a dish of assertive other ingredients. Cans of red kidney beans are an excellent standby as half the work is done for you. Use them in your favourite chilli con carne recipe or as in this recipe.

■

SERVES 4

4 rashers of belly pork

1 large onion

1 tablespoon vegetable oil

1–2 teaspoons chilli powder

two 397 g (14 oz) cans red kidney beans

397 g (14 oz) can tomatoes

generous splash of red wine

1 tablespoon wholegrain mustard

salt and pepper

■

1 Using scissors, cut the rind off the pork. Skin and chop the onion.

2 Heat the oil in a flameproof casserole dish and fry the onion for 2–3 minutes until soft. Stir in the chilli powder, drained kidney beans, tomatoes with their juice, red wine, mustard, salt and pepper.

3 Place the pork rashers on top of the mixture. Cook, uncovered, at 220°C (425°F) mark 7 for 30–35 minutes until the pork is tender. Accompany with boiled rice or chunks of French bread.

MONKFISH PROVENCALE

Monkfish has a lovely firm white flesh which does not fall apart when cooked. Its delicate flavour combines beautifully with a Provençale sauce.

■

SERVES 2

1 medium onion

2 tablespoons vegetable oil

2 large garlic cloves

275 g (10 oz) monkfish

397 g (14 oz) can tomatoes

splash of dry white wine

bouquet garni

salt and pepper

■

1 Skin and slice the onion. Heat the oil in a flameproof casserole, add the onion and crush in the garlic. Cook until golden.

2 Meanwhile, skin and cut the fish into cubes, removing the central bone. When the onions are cooked, push to one side of the pan. Add the fish and cook for 1–2 minutes on each side until firm and slightly coloured.

3 Add the tomatoes with their juice, the wine, bouquet garni, salt and pepper. Simmer gently, uncovered, for 10–15 minutes until tender. Serve with boiled potatoes and sliced courgettes.

■ TO COOK IN A MICROWAVE: Put the oil, sliced onion and crushed garlic in a large bowl. Cook on HIGH for 4–5 minutes until softened. Meanwhile, prepare the fish. Add the tomatoes, wine, bouquet garni, salt and pepper to the bowl and cook, uncovered, on HIGH for 8 minutes until boiling and reduced slightly. Stir in the fish and cook on HIGH for 4–5 minutes or until the fish is tender, stirring once.

POACHED PLAICE IN VERMOUTH

Vermouth is a fortified wine which is given its flavour by an infusion of herbs. No wonder then that this dish has more character than when simply cooked in white wine.

■

SERVES 2
knob of butter or margarine
2 spring onions
2 tablespoons dry vermouth
1 tablespoon lemon juice
small garlic clove
pinch of dill
green peppercorns
salt and pepper
2 plaice fillets, each weighing 175 g (6 oz), skinned
lemon slices, to garnish

■

1 Butter a shallow dish that will just hold the fish. Slice the spring onions and put in the dish with the vermouth, lemon juice, the crushed garlic, dill, a few peppercorns, crushed, salt and pepper. Marinate the fish in this mixture for 10 minutes, turning once.

2 Cover and cook in the oven at 180°C (350°F) mark 4 for 15–20 minutes until tender. Garnish with lemon slices. Serve with creamed potatoes and spinach with nutmeg.

■ TO COOK IN A MICROWAVE: Cover the prepared dish and microwave on HIGH for 4 minutes until tender.

SINGAPORE NOODLES

Here, rice noodles are combined with shrimps, mushrooms and fresh chicken. You can buy the ingredients listed below from Chinese food stores and specialist food shops.

■

SERVES 2
2 tablespoons dried shrimps
4 Chinese dried mushrooms
2.5 cm (1 inch) piece of root ginger
1 cooked chicken breast
100 g (4 oz) rice stick noodles
50 g (2 oz) cooked peeled prawns
4 tablespoons vegetable oil
1 medium onion, skinned and chopped
1 garlic clove, skinned and finely chopped
4 spring onions, trimmed and finely sliced
½ teaspoon curry powder
2 tablespoons soy sauce
1 tablespoon dry sherry
1 tablespoon hoisin sauce

■

1 Put the shrimps and mushrooms in a small bowl. Cover with boiling water and leave to soak for 20–30 minutes until soft.
2 Meanwhile, peel and grate the ginger. Remove the skin and any bones and cut the chicken into shreds. Put the noodles in a large bowl, pour over boiling water and leave to soak for 2 minutes, then drain well.
3 Drain the shrimps and mushrooms, reserving the liquid. Finely shred the mushrooms, discarding the stems.
4 Heat the oil in a wok or large frying pan, then add the mushrooms, shrimps, onion, garlic and ginger. Stir-fry for 2 minutes.
5 Add the spring onions, chicken, prawns, curry powder and 3 tablespoons of the reserved soaking liquid and stir-fry for a 2 minutes. Add the noodles and toss well together. Add the soy sauce, sherry and hoisin sauce and toss again, then serve hot.

CHEESE AND SPINACH LASAGNE

Sheets of lasagne which require no precooking are a useful standby to keep in the store cupboard. They not only save time, but also make the task of assembling a lasagne far easier.

■

SERVES 4
two 300 g (10.6 oz) packets frozen leaf spinach, thawed
175 g (6 oz) ricotta or cottage cheese
small handful of pine kernels (optional)
whole nutmeg
salt and pepper
8 sheets oven-ready plain or green lasagne
25 g (1 oz) butter or margarine
4 tablespoons flour
568 ml (1 pint) milk
75 g (3 oz) mature Cheddar cheese

■

1 Put the thawed spinach in a sieve and squeeze out the liquid with the back of a spoon.

2 Mix the spinach with half of the ricotta, the pine kernels, if used, a few gratings of nutmeg and salt and pepper. Spoon half of the spinach mixture over the base of the dish. Cover with half of the pasta. Repeat these layers once more.

3 Put the butter, flour and milk into a saucepan. Slowly bring to the boil, whisking continuously, until the sauce thickens, then simmer for 1–2 minutes. Grate half of the Cheddar cheese into the hot sauce and add the remaining ricotta, salt and pepper.

4 Pour the sauce over the lasagne. Grate the remaining cheese on top. Bake at 200°C (400°F) mark 6 for 20–30 minutes until bubbling.

■ TO COOK IN A MICROWAVE: The sauce can be prepared in a microwave. Put the butter, flour and milk in a medium bowl and stir together. Cook on HIGH for 5–6 minutes until the sauce has boiled and thickened, whisking frequently. Complete the sauce as in step 3.

CRANACHAN

This delectable Scottish pudding consists of toasted oatmeal, fresh cream, honey and a liberal splash of whisky, combined with the sharp full taste of raspberries. It actually only takes about 20 minutes to prepare, during the remaining time it is left to chill.

■

SERVES 4
50 g (2 oz) medium oatmeal
300 ml (½ pint) double cream
4 tablespoons honey
3 tablespoons whisky
350 g (12 oz) fresh raspberries

■

1 Spread the oatmeal in a grill pan and toast until golden brown, turning occasionally with a spoon. Leave to cool.
2 Meanwhile, whisk the cream until just standing in soft peaks, then stir in the honey, whisky and cool oatmeal.
3 Reserve a few for decoration, then layer up the remaining raspberries and the cream mixture in 4 tall glasses.
4 Chill in the refrigerator for about 20 minutes. Decorate each helping with the reserved raspberries before serving.

CHEWY CHOCOLATE BROWNIES

Serve these moist, munchy Chocolate Brownies warm, as a dessert with real vanilla ice cream. You can also serve them with hot Chocolate Sauce. Make the recipe on page 32 whilst the Brownies are being baked. If you have any over, leave until cold, then store in an airtight tin and eat them for tea.

■

MAKES 6
100 g (4 oz) butter or margarine, plus extra for greasing
75 g (3 oz) plain white flour
175 g (6 oz) dark soft brown sugar
25 g (1 oz) cocoa powder
pinch of salt
2 eggs
1 teaspoon vanilla flavouring
75 g (3 oz) chopped walnuts

■

1 Grease a 18 cm (7 inch) square cake tin. Put all the ingredients in a bowl and, using an electric whisk, beat well until evenly combined.

2 Turn the mixture into the tin and level the surface. Bake at 180°C (350°F) mark 4 for about 25 minutes until just set. The mixture should still wobble slightly in the centre.

3 Leave in the cake tin for 5–10 minutes, then cut into 6 pieces. Serve with ice cream and or chocolate sauce.

■ TO COOK IN A MICROWAVE: Grease a shallow 23 × 12.5 cm (9 × 5 inch) dish. Prepare the mixture, adding 3 tablespoons milk. Turn into the dish and level the surface. Cover with absorbent kitchen paper, stand on a rack and cook on MEDIUM for 10–12 minutes until well risen, firm to the touch, but still slightly moist in the middle. Leave to stand in the dish for 10 minutes, then cut into 6 pieces. Serve warm.

CHAPTER 6

C O O K   A H E A D

VICHYSSOISE

Though made from the humble potato, nothing could make a more sophisticated starter to a summer meal than this chilled leek and potato soup. A good, rich home-made stock is ideal but if you have to fall back on a stock cube to save time, use less of the cube than recommended and do not add salt.

■

SERVES 4
4 leeks
1 onion
2 potatoes
50 g (2 oz) butter
1 litre (1¾ pints) chicken stock
salt and pepper
200 ml (7 fl oz) single cream
fresh chives, to garnish

■

1 TO PREPARE: Trim, slice and wash the leeks. Skin and slice the onion. Peel and thinly slice the potatoes.

2 Melt the butter in a saucepan, add the leeks and onion and cook gently for about 10 minutes, until soft but not coloured. Add the stock and potatoes and bring to the boil.

3 Lower the heat, add salt and pepper to taste and cover. Simmer for about 30 minutes until the vegetables are soft.

4 Allow to cool slightly, then turn into a food processor and blend until smooth or push through a sieve to form a purée. Pour into a large serving bowl and stir in the cream. Chill for at least 4 hours.

5 TO SERVE: Whisk the soup to ensure an even consistency. Pour into individual bowls and snip fresh chives on top to garnish.

■ TO COOK IN A MICROWAVE: Prepare the vegetables. Put the butter into a large bowl and cook on HIGH for 1 minute until melted. Stir in the leeks and onion. Cover and cook on HIGH for 5–7 minutes until they are softened. Add the stock, potatoes, salt and pepper and cook on HIGH for 15–17 minutes until the vegetables are very soft, stirring frequently. Complete the recipe.

CEVICHE

This is a Mexican recipe in which the acidic lime juice pickles and tenderises the fish so that it does not need cooking. To save extra time, ask your fishmonger to skin the fish for you.

■

SERVES 6 as a starter, 3 as a light dish
450 g (1 lb) haddock or cod fillets
salt and pepper
1 medium onion
2 garlic cloves
1 dried red chilli
juice of 6 large limes or 5 lemons
1 avocado
1 bunch of fresh coriander

■

1 TO PREPARE: Skin the fish fillets, then cut into thin strips, removing any bones. Put the strips in a bowl and season with plenty of salt and pepper.
2 Skin and finely slice the onion. Skin and finely chop the garlic. Add to the fish, crumble in the chilli, then pour over the lime or lemon juice, making sure that the fish is covered.
3 Cover and leave in the refrigerator to marinate for 8 hours or overnight.
4 TO SERVE: Halve the avocado, peel and remove the stone. Slice the flesh crossways. Arrange the slices around a serving dish. Drain the fish from the marinade, (it should look 'cooked', and white and no longer transparent) and pile the fish in the centre of the dish. Finely chop the coriander leaves and sprinkle over the top of the Ceviche. Serve this dish with a simple tomato salad if serving as a light meal.

CHICKEN SATAY

■

SERVES 4
100 g (4 oz) creamed coconut
6 tablespoons crunchy peanut butter
3 tablespoons lemon juice
2 tablespoons soy sauce
large pinch of chilli powder
4 chicken breast fillets, skinned
2 tablespoons vegetable oil
2 garlic cloves
1 tablespoon ground turmeric
1 teaspoon 5-spice powder
1 teaspoon coriander seeds
1 teaspoon cumin seeds

■

1 TO PREPARE: Crumble 50 g (2 oz) of the coconut into a saucepan. Add the peanut butter, 1 tablespoon of the lemon juice, 1 tablespoon of the soy sauce, chilli powder and 300 ml (½ pint) water. Bring slowly to the boil, stirring, then simmer for 3–5 minutes until the sauce has thickened. Turn into a small serving bowl.
2 Cut the chicken into small chunks and put in a bowl. Put the remaining coconut, remaining lemon juice, remaining soy sauce and ingredients in a food processor and work until smooth.
3 Pour over the chicken. Cover; marinate in the refrigerator for 8 hours.
4 TO SERVE: Thread the chicken on to 8 oiled skewers and grill for 10–15 minutes, turning frequently and basting with any remaining marinade. Serve hot, with the sauce for dipping.
■ **TO COOK IN A MICROWAVE:** To make the sauce, complete step 1, using a medium bowl. Cook on HIGH for 4–5 minutes until the sauce boils, stirring frequently. Complete steps 3 and 4.
■ **TO SERVE:** Thread the chicken on to 8 wooden kebab sticks. Place in a shallow dish and pour over any remaining marinade. cover and cook on HIGH for 10–12 minutes or until the chicken is cooked, turning at least twice. Serve hot, accompanied by the sauce.

TERIYAKI

This Japanese dish is ideal for entertaining. Teriyaki sauce is used extensively in the cooking of Japan. Chicken and prawns are often marinated in the sauce and sometimes pork or cubes of firm-fleshed white fish. For a special dinner party meal, you can cook a selection of different meats, fish and shellfish in this way. In Japan, Teriyaki is served together with many other dishes – there are no separate courses in a Japanese meal. However, for a Western style Japanese dinner party you can serve a soup to start with, followed by Teriyaki as a main course dish. Boiled rice or noodles and stir-fried vegetables make suitable accompaniments.

■

SERVES 4
1 garlic clove
2.5 cm (1 inch) piece of fresh root ginger
8 tablespoons soy sauce
6 tablespoons mirin (Japanese sweet rice wine) or sweet sherry
4 tablespoons sugar
pepper
700–900 g (1–1½ lb) fillet steak
2 tablespoons vegetable oil

■

1 TO PREPARE: Crush the garlic into a bowl, then peel and crush in the ginger. Add the soy sauce, mirin, sugar and pepper to taste, then whisk them with a fork until well combined.
2 Trim any fat off the steak, then cut into cubes about 1 cm (½ inch) thick. Add to the bowl and coat in the marinade. Cover and marinate for 2–3 hours, or in the refrigerator overnight.
3 TO SERVE: Soak 12 bamboo skewers in water for 15 minutes or oil 4 flat kebab skewers. Thread the cubes of steak on to the skewers. Brush the meat with oil, then cook under a preheated hot grill for 4–8 minutes according to how well done you like your steak. Turn the skewers frequently during grilling and brush with more oil and any remaining marinade. Serve immediately.

Osso Bucco

■

SERVES 4

1 onion

50 g (2 oz) butter

1 tablespoon olive oil

4–8 ossi buchi (veal shin, hind cut), sawn into 5 cm (2 inch) pieces weighing about 1.75 kg (3½ lb)

50 g (2 oz) plain flour

salt and pepper

300 ml (½ pint) dry white wine

300 ml (½ pint) chicken stock

1 garlic clove

finely grated rind of 1 lemon

3 tablespoons chopped fresh parsley

■

1 TO PREPARE: Skin and finely chop the onion. Melt the butter with the oil in a flameproof casserole, add the onion and fry gently for 5 minutes until soft but not coloured.

2 Coat the veal in the flour seasoned with salt and pepper. Add to the casserole and fry for about 10 minutes until browned.

3 Pour over the wine and boil rapidly for 5 minutes, then add the chicken stock.

4 Cover the pan tightly and simmer for 1½–2 hours, turning the meat occasionally. When the meat is cooked, remove the pan from the heat and leave to cool. Store in the refrigerator until required.

5 TO SERVE: Bring to the boil, then simmer for 10–15 minutes to heat through. Meanwhile, skin and finely chop the garlic and mix with the lemon rind and the parsley. Sprinkle over the Osso Bucco and serve hot. Accompany by yellow saffron rice; dissolve a pinch of saffron strands in 1 tablespoon boiling water. With a fork, half stir through boiled white rice so that it is streaked with yellow. It looks pretty and effective with hardly any effort.

HAM AND MUSHROOM GOUGERE

■

SERVES 3–4

90 g (3½ oz) butter or margarine, plus extra for greasing

90 g (3½ oz) plain white flour

2 eggs

50 g (2 oz) Cheddar or Red Leicester cheese

salt and pepper

450 g (1 lb) can lean cooked ham

1 medium onion

100 g (4 oz) button mushrooms

300 ml (½ pint) milk

2 tablespoons chopped fresh parsley

■

1 TO PREPARE: Make the choux pastry by putting 50 g (2 oz) of the butter or margarine and 150 ml (¼ pint) water in a saucepan. Heat gently until the butter has melted, then bring to the boil.

2 Immediately the water boils, remove from the heat and quickly tip in 65 g (2½ oz) of the flour. Beat with a wooden spoon until the mixture is smooth and just leaves the sides of the pan.

3 Allow to cool for 1–2 minutes, then gradually beat in the eggs, keeping the mixture stiff. Grate the cheese into the sauce and add salt and pepper. Store in the refrigerator.

4 To make the filling, trim the ham of any jelly, then cut into cubes. Skin and thinly slice the onion. Slice the mushrooms.

5 Melt the remaining butter or margarine in a saucepan, add the onion and mushrooms and cook, stirring, for 2–3 minutes. Add the remaining flour and cook for a further minute.

6 Remove from the heat and gradually stir in the milk. Bring to the boil and cook until thickened. Stir in the ham, parsley, salt and pepper. Store in the refrigerator.

7 TO SERVE: Grease a shallow 1.7 litre (3 pint) ovenproof dish. Spoon the choux pastry around the edges, then pour the sauce into the centre. Bake at 200°C (400°F) mark 6 for 35–40 minutes until the pastry is well risen, browned and firm to the touch.

PERSIAN LAMB AND
APRICOT STEW

This Persian dish is rich and spicy. It takes only 15 minutes to prepare and can then be left to simmer. All you need do is stir it occasionally as you pass. Left to cool and then reheated the following day, the spices have time to mature and the flavour improve. Serve with boiled rice which you can cook while reheating the stew.

■

SERVES 8
2.3 kg (5 lb) boned leg of lamb
1 large onion
225 g (8 oz) no-soak dried apricots
1 tablespoon vegetable oil
1 teaspoon ground coriander
1 teaspoon ground cumin
½ teaspoon ground cinnamon
25 g (1 oz) ground almonds
salt and pepper

■

1 TO PREPARE: Trim the meat of fat and cut into 2.5 cm (1 inch) cubes. Skin and chop the onion. Cut the apricots in half.

2 Heat the oil in a large saucepan. Add the lamb and onion and cook for 10 minutes, stirring until lightly browned.

3 Stir in the spices, almonds, salt and pepper. Add 300 ml (½ pint) water and the apricots. Cover and simmer for 1½ hours or until the lamb is tender, stirring occasionally. Leave to cool, then cover and refrigerate until required.

4 TO SERVE: Bring slowly to the boil, then lower the heat, cover and simmer for 5–10 minutes until heated through. Serve hot with boiled rice.

RICH PHEASANT CASSEROLE

The more simply game is cooked, the better, and older birds,
which are likely to be tough, benefit from being casseroled.
Here a brace of pheasants is cooked slowly in port and stock to
produce a delicious casserole that reheats very well the
following day.

■

SERVES 4
2 medium onions
2 tablespoons vegetable oil
50 g (2 oz) butter or margarine
a brace of oven-ready pheasants
150 ml (¼ pint) port
300 ml (½ pint) beef stock
1 bay leaf
salt and pepper

■

1 TO PREPARE: Skin and slice the onions. Heat the oil and butter in
a large flameproof casserole and fry the pheasants for about 5
minutes until brown all over. Remove from the casserole and
transfer to a plate.
2 Add the onions and fry for 5 minutes until softened. Return the
pheasants to the casserole.
3 Stir in the port and stock, add the bay leaf, salt and pepper.
Bring to the boil, then cover and cook in the oven at 170°C (325°F)
mark 3 for about 1¼ hours until the pheasants are tender. Leave to
cool, then refrigerate until required.
4 TO SERVE: Either bring slowly to the boil on top of the cooker,
then lower the heat, cover and simmer for 30 minutes until
heated through, or reheat in the oven at 200°C (400°F) mark 6 for
about 40 minutes. Serve hot with mashed or small baked potatoes
and Brussels sprouts.

BLACKBERRY MOUSSES

These look so pretty. Make them in advance to serve as a light summer dessert.

∎

SERVES 6
150 ml (¼ pint) natural yogurt
213 g (7½ oz) can blackberries in unsweetened fruit juice
2 tablespoons caster sugar
3 teaspoons gelatine
300 ml (½ pint) whipping cream

∎

1 TO PREPARE: Put the yogurt in a bowl, add 6 tablespoons of juice from the can of blackberries and the sugar and stir well together. Reserve the blackberries and remaining juice.

2 Sprinkle the gelatine over 4 tablespoons cold water in a small bowl and leave to soak for 1 minute. Place over a pan of gently boiling water and stir until the gelatine is dissolved. Allow to cool slightly, then stir into the yogurt mixture.

3 Whisk the cream until stiff, then fold into the mixture.

4 Rinse the insides of 6 ramekin dishes under cold water and drain. Spoon in the mousse mixture and level the surface. Put in the refrigerator to set for at least 4 hours, or overnight.

5 TO SERVE: Run a knife around the edge of each ramekin dish and turn out the mousses on to individual plates. Spoon the reserved blackberries on top, then serve.

∎ TO COOK IN A MICROWAVE: The gelatine can be dissolved in the microwave. Place the bowl containing the gelatine and water in the oven and cook on HIGH for 30 seconds–1 minute until dissolved, stirring occasionally. Do not let it boil.

CHAPTER 7

BASIC RECIPES

SHORTCRUST PASTRY

A food processor makes light work of shortcrust pastry and not only is it very quick, but the results are very good. For convenience, make up a large batch of rubbed in mixture and store in a polythene bag in the refrigerator for several weeks. The water can then be added just before use. It is most important not to over-process the mixture as a food processor works in seconds. For even rubbing in, process by operating in short bursts rather than by letting the machine run continuously. Make sure that you know the capacity of your food processor and never overload the processor bowl. If making a very large quantity of pastry, make it in two batches.

QUANTITY: When a recipe requires 225 g (8 oz) pastry, this refers to the weight of flour. For any quantity of shortcrust pastry, always use half fat to flour.

■

225 g (8 oz) plain flour
pinch of salt
50 g (2 oz) butter or block margarine
50 g (2 oz) lard
about 8 teaspoons cold water

■

1 Put the flour and salt in the bowl of a food processor, fitted with a metal blade. Cut the fat into small pieces and add to the flour. Mix, using a pulse action, until the mixture resembles fine breadcrumbs. If wished, the mixture can be stored in the refrigerator at this stage.

2 Sprinkle the water on the flour and mix, using a pulse action, until a dough begins to form.

3 Mix briefly until the dough forms a ball and leaves the side of the bowl. If time allows, pastry benefits from being left to rest for about 30 minutes, wrapped in greaseproof paper or foil in the refrigerator. It can be stored this way for up to 2 days.

4 Roll out the dough out on a lightly floured surface with a lightly floured rolling pin and shape as required. Bake in the oven at 200–220°C (400–425°F) mark 6–7 or as the recipe directs, until lightly browned.

CRUMBLE TOPPINGS

Both savoury and sweet crumble can be used in a variety of ways, and, as with shortcrust pastry, it is useful to have a quantity of basic mixture stored in the refrigerator. The basic mixture is half the quantity of butter or margarine mixed into flour as for shortcrust pastry.

■

SAVOURY CRUMBLE: To the basic mixture, add salt and pepper, dried or chopped fresh herbs and grated cheese.

Sprinkle over savoury cooked minced beef or lamb, a vegetable hot pot or fricassee dish. Bake at 200°C (400°F) mark 6 for about 30 minutes until golden brown.

FOR SWEET CRUMBLE: To the basic mixture, add half the quantity of sugar to the flour, then add a handful of rolled oats, grated orange or lemon rind, chopped nuts, desiccated coconut, ground cinnamon or mixed spice.

Sprinkle over prepared fresh fruit such as apples, rhubarb, plums, blackberries or gooseberries or a can of fruit and bake at 200°C (400°F) mark 6 for about 30 minutes until golden brown.

SPONGE TOPPING: Making a sponge mixture by the all-in-one method is wonderfully quick and easy to prepare and makes an excellent topping for a hot pudding. You will need 100 g (4 oz) each of self-raising flour, soft tub margarine and caster sugar, plus 1 teaspoon baking powder, 2 eggs and 1 tablespoon milk.

Sift the flour and baking powder into a large bowl. Add all the other ingredients then simply beat together with a wooden spoon or electric whisk for 2–3 minutes, until well blended and slightly glossy.

Spoon over prepared fruit such as apples (for an Eve's Pudding) rhubarb, gooseberries, plums, blackberries or other soft fruits or a can of fruit. Bake at 170°C (325°F) mark 3 for 30 minutes until the sponge mixture is golden brown.

HOLLANDAISE SAUCE

This is a classic sauce to serve with salmon and other fish dishes, asparagus or broccoli, egg and chicken dishes. Made in a blender or food processor, it is almost foolproof and there is no tricky, time-consuming whisking and cooking over boiling water involved.

■

SERVES 4

2 egg yolks

salt and pepper

2 tablespoons wine vinegar

100 g (4 oz) butter

■

1 Using a food processor, fit the metal blade or whisk. Put the egg yolks, salt and pepper in the bowl and mix well.
2 Put the vinegar and 1 tablespoon water in a small pan and boil until reduced to about 1 tablespoon. At the same time melt the butter in another pan and bring to the boil.
3 With the machine on, add the boiling vinegar then butter in a slow, steady stream through the feeder tube. Mix well then turn into a warmed serving bowl or jug. It should be warm rather than hot when served.
4 If not serving immediately, the sauce can be turned into a bowl and kept warm over warm (not hot) water for about 15 minutes, whisking occasionally.

FRENCH DRESSING

(Sauce Vinaigrette)

Salad dressings are often thrown together very casually with indifferent ingredients. This is a shame, for the taste of the dressing will determine at least half of the taste of the finished salad. Try to choose your oil for its flavour: olive, walnut or hazelnut oil if you like a strong flavour; sunflower or groundnut oil if you like a clean, neutral taste. Be careful, too, about your choice of vinegar, which should be wine, herb, flavoured or cider vinegar, never malt. Lemon juice may be used instead of vinegar, or try a mixture of half and half. Remember the old adage: you need four people to make a good dressing – a spendthrift for the oil, a miser for the vinegar, a wise man for the salt, and a madman for the pepper. Imitate each in turn and you won't go far wrong. Always keep a quantity of French Dressing in the refrigerator so that it is there when you need it. It will keep for many months. Make and store it in a bottle or screw-topped jar.

∎

MAKES 16 TABLESPOONS

NOTE The proportion of oil to vinegar can be varied according to taste. Here it is in the ratio of three to one. Use less oil if a sharper dressing is preferred.

12 tablespoons oil (see above)

4 tablespoons vinegar or lemon juice (see above)

pinch of sugar

1 teaspoon mustard, eg wholegrain, Dijon, French or mustard powder

salt and pepper

∎

1 Put all the ingredients in a bottle or screw-topped jar and shake until well blended. The oil separates out on standing, so shake the dressing again immediately before use.

WALNUT DRESSING

This Italian salad dressing is quickly made in a food processor. It can be stored for up to 1 week in a covered bowl or screw-topped jar in the refrigerator. Use as an alternative to French dressing for green salads.

■

MAKES 225 ml (8 fl oz)
1 small slice of wholemeal bread
40 g (1½ oz) walnuts
2 teaspoons lemon juice
1 garlic clove, skinned
salt and pepper
200 ml (7 fl oz) olive oil

■

1 Remove the crusts from the bread and soak the bread in cold water for a few minutes.
2 Squeeze out the excess moisture and place the bread in the bowl of a food processor, fitted with a metal blade.
3 Add the walnuts, lemon juice, garlic and salt and pepper and work until the mixture is very finely ground.
4 Gradually add the oil through the feeder tube, while the machine is still running, until it is all incorporated. Stir well before use.

INDEX